FAC
GR

FACING GRIEF

Counsel for Mourners

John Flavel

And when the Lord saw her, he had compassion on her,
and said unto her, Weep not (*Luke* 7:13).

THE BANNER OF TRUTH TRUST

THE BANNER OF TRUTH TRUST
3 Murrayfield Road, Edinburgh EH12 6EL, UK
P.O. Box 621, Carlisle, PA 17013, USA

*

First published 1674
as *A Token for Mourners*

Previously published in
The Works of John Flavel, vol. 5
(1820; repr. Banner of Truth Trust, 1968)

This reset edition
© The Banner of Truth Trust, 2010

ISBN-13: 978 1 84871 069 6

*

Typeset in 10.5/14 pt Sabon at the
Banner of Truth Trust, Edinburgh
Printed in the USA by
Versa Press, Inc.,
East Peoria, IL

Contents

Foreword

JOHN FLAVEL (1627–91) was a minister of the gospel in the south of England — in Salisbury first, and then mainly in Dartmouth. Living through tumultuous times in England, Flavel faced even more tumultuous times in his own life. Like his Master, he lived a life acquainted with grief. He was one of the thousands of ministers of the Church of England who resigned their living in the Great Ejection of 1662. His parents both died of the plague in 1665 under tragic circumstances. (They were imprisoned by enemies at the infamously infected Newgate Prison, presumably in order to cause their deaths.) Flavel saw the death of his child, and three wives. After only two years of marriage, his first wife, Joanna, died in childbirth, along with their first child. He remarried, and also grieved the loss of Elizabeth, his second wife. Having remarried again — to Agnes — he also lost her. He was survived by his fourth wife, Dorothy.

In 1674, two years after his second wife had died, John Flavel published *A Token for Mourners,* based upon advice he gave to a woman who had lost her only child.

In this work, Flavel meditates on the words of Luke 7:13, 'And when the Lord saw her, he had compassion on her, and said unto her, Weep not.' From this verse Flavel helps the reader to think about sorrowing that is 'moderate' and 'immoderate'. He spells out what is permitted and appropriate for a Christian, and what is not. He even has a section of advice to non-Christians who are mourning a loss. Most of the work, however, offers comfort to 'godly mourners'. This book is full of Scripture, counsel, warning, and wisdom gained from prayerful reflection on the personal experience of affliction in loss and grief.

For the next 150 years Flavel's *Token* was printed and re-printed in England and America. The times demanded that the heart-breaking experience of the loss of children be faced by most parents. And generations of Christian parents found comfort through this little book.

I first became acquainted with this work when a couple in our congregation was called to go through the dark valley of losing their first child. Flavel's *Token* helped them to trust God for good through the affliction and grief. It helped them to fix their eyes on Jesus, the Author and Perfecter of their faith when they needed such help most.

I had owned this work for decades — but it was hidden at the back of volume five of the collected *Works* of Flavel. I had read some of his more theological works, and the 'Puritan Paperback' edition of Flavel's *The Mystery of Providence* — one of my favorite Puritan works. Now republished as *Facing Grief: Counsel for Mourners*, this new edition makes Flavel's *Token for Mourners* more accessible. By publishing it separately, and in a lightly-edited form, the Banner of Truth Trust has allowed the work once again to take the form in which it knew such popularity among grieving Christians for 150 years — a small book, published on its own — the right size for carrying, and reading alone, slowly, and with meditation, reflection, and prayer.

May reading these pages prayerfully remind you, believer, of our certain hope in Christ. May you be protected from danger as you are led to Christ during your time of grief. May you embrace the promises that we have in Christ, and find your heart pastored by this faithful minister of God's Word.

MARK DEVER
Washington D.C.
December 2009

Epistle Dedicatory[1]

DEAR FRIENDS

*T*he double tie of nature and grace, besides the many endearing passages that for many years have linked and glued our affections so intimately, cannot but beget in me a tender sympathy with you under all your troubles; and make me say of every affliction which befalls you, 'Half mine'. I find it is with our affections as with the strings of musical instruments exactly set at the same pitch, if one be touched the other trembles, though it be at some distance.

It is not my design to exasperate your troubles, but to heal them; and for that purpose have I sent you these papers, which I hope may be of use to you and many others in your condition, since they are the after-fruits of my own troubles; things that I have not commended to you from another hand, but which I have, in some measure, proved and tasted in my own trials.

---

[1] The original inscription read: 'To his dearly beloved brother and sister, Mr J. C. and Mrs E. C., the Author wisheth Grace, Mercy and Peace.'

I have only a few things to desire for and from you:

1. *That you will not be too hasty to get off the yoke which God has put upon your neck.* Desire not to be delivered from your sorrows one moment before God's time. Let patience have its perfect work; that comfort, which comes in God's way and season may remain and do you good.

2. *I desire, that though you and your afflictions had a sad meeting, yet you and they may have a comfortable parting.* If they effect that upon your hearts which God sent them for, I doubt not but you will give them a fair testimony when they go off. How sweet it is to hear the afflicted soul say, when God is loosing his bands, 'It is good for me that I have been afflicted!'

3. *I heartily wish that these searching afflictions may make the most satisfying discoveries, that you may now see more of the evil of sin, the vanity of the creature, and the fulness of Christ.* Afflictions put the soul upon searching and trying its way. 'Blessed is the man whom God chastens, and teaches out of his law' (*Psa.* 94:12).

4. *I wish that all the love and delight you bestowed upon your little one may now be placed to your greater advantage upon Jesus Christ;* and that the stream of your affection to him may be so much the stronger as there are now fewer channels for it to be divided into.

5. *That you may be strengthened with all might in the inner man to all patience, that the peace of God may keep your hearts and minds.* Labour to attain to a meek submission to the rod of your Father. The soul grows wise by sitting still and quiet under the rod.

6. *Lastly, My heart's desire and prayer to God for you is, that you may die daily to all visible enjoyments, and by these frequent converses with death in your family, you may be prepared for your own change and dissolution when it shall come.*

O friends! how many graves have you and I seen opened for our dear relations? How oft has death come up into your windows and summoned the delight of your eyes? It is but a little while and we shall go to them; we and they are distinguished but by short intervals.

Our dear parents are gone, our lovely and desirable children are gone, our bosom relations, that were as our own souls, are gone. And do not all these warning-knocks at our doors acquaint us that we must prepare to follow shortly after them?

Oh, that by these things our own death might be both more easy and familiar to us! The oftener it visits us, the better we should be acquainted with it; and the more of our beloved relations it removes before us, the less of either snare or entanglement remains for us, when our own turn comes.

My dear friends, I beseech you, for religion's sake, for your own sake, and for my sake, whose comfort is, in great part, bound up in your prosperity and welfare, that you apply believingly these Scripture-consolations and directions, which, in some haste, I have gathered for your use; and the God of all consolation be with you.

I am,

Your most endeared Brother,

JOHN FLAVEL

I

The Text Explained

*And when the Lord saw her, he had compassion
on her, and said unto her, Weep not.*

LUKE 7:13

To be above the stroke of passions is a condition
equal to angels; to be in a state of sorrow without
the sense of sorrow is a disposition beneath beasts;
but duly to regulate our sorrows and bound our passions
under the rod is the wisdom, duty, and excellency of a
Christian. He who is without natural affections is deserv-
edly ranked among the worst of heathens; and he who
is able rightly to manage them deserves to be numbered
with the best of Christians. Though when we are sanctified we put on the divine nature, yet, till we are glorified,
we put not off the infirmities of our human nature.

While we are within reach of troubles, we cannot be
without the danger, and ought not to be without the
fear, of sin; and it is as hard for us to escape sin, being in
adversity, as becalming in prosperity.

How likely we are to transgress the bounds, both of reason and religion, under a sharp affliction, appears, as in most men's experience, so in this woman's example, to whose excessive sorrow Christ puts a stop in the text: 'He saw her, and had compassion on her, and said to her, Weep not.'

The lamentations and wailings of this distressed mother moved the tender compassions of the Lord in observing them, and stirred up more pity in his heart for her than could be in her heart for her dear and only son.

In these words, we are to consider both the condition of the woman, and the counsel of Christ with respect unto it.

The Condition of the Woman
First, The condition of this woman, which appears to be very dolorous and distressed; her groans and tears moved and melted the very heart of Christ to hear and observe them: 'When he saw her he had compassion on her.'

How sad an hour it was with her when Christ met her appears by what is so distinctly remarked by the Evangelist in verse 12 where it is said, 'Now when they came near to the gate of the city, behold, there was a dead man carried out, the only son of his mother, and she was a widow, and much people of the city was with her.'

In this one verse, several heart-piercing circumstances of this affliction are noted.

1. It was *the death of a son.*[1] To bury a child, any child,

---

[1] φιλιας μεγιστος δεσμος ειναι τεκνων γοναι, i.e., To be parents to children is the firmest tie of affection. *Græc. Com.*

rends the heart of a tender parent; for what are children, but the parent multiplied? A child is a part of the parent made up in another skin. But to lay a son in the grave, a son who continues the name and supports the family; this was always reckoned a very great affliction.

2. This son was not carried from the cradle to the coffin, nor stripped out of his baby-clothes to be wrapped in his grave-clothes. Had he died in his infancy, before he had engaged affection or raised expectation, the affliction might not have been so pungent and cutting as now it was. Death smote the son in the flower and prime of his time. He was *a man* (says the Evangelist) verse 12, *a young man* (as Christ calls him) verse 14; he was now arrived at that age which made him capable of yielding his mother all that comfort which had been the expectation and hope of many years, and the reward and fruit of many cares and labours; yet then, when the endearments were greatest, and her hopes highest, even in the flower of his age, he is cut off.[1]

Thus Basil bewailed the death of his son:

I once had a son, who was a young man, my only successor, the solace of my age, the glory of his kind, the prop of my family, arrived to the endearing age; then was he snatched away from me by death, whose lovely voice but a little before I heard, who lately was a pleasant spectacle to his parent.

Reader, if this has been your own condition, as it has

---

[1] He died in his youth, and was therefore the more to be lamented, because he was cut off in the flower of his age , unto which he was conducted from a child, by the great care and labour of his parents. *Dion. Cat. on the place.*

been his who writes it, I need say no more to convince you that it was a sorrowful state indeed that Christ met this tender mother in.[1]

3. And, which is yet more, he was not only a son, but an *only son*; so you find, in verse 12; 'He was the only son of his mother'; one in whom all her hopes and comforts were bound up.[2] For, *Omnis in Ascanio stat chari cura parentis* [All the care of the fond parent stands in Ascanius], Virgil. All her affections were contracted into this one object. If we have ever so many children, we know not which of them to spare; if they stand like olive plants about our tables, it would grieve us to see the least twig amongst them broken down. But surely the death of one out of many is much more tolerable than all in one.[3]

Hence it is noted in Scripture as the greatest of earthly sorrows, 'O daughter of my people, gird you with sackcloth, and wallow yourself in ashes: make you mourning as for an only son, most bitter lamentation' (*Jer.* 6:26). Yea, so deep and penetrating is this grief that the Holy Ghost borrows it to express the deepest spiritual troubles by it: 'They shall mourn for him [namely Christ] whom they have pierced, as one mourns for his only son' (*Zech.* 12:10).

---

[1] Flavel was no stranger to bereavement. He buried three of his four wives, and a newborn infant alongside one of them. His fourth wife survived him.

[2] She would have borne his death more patiently had he not been an only son; or if she had but another left behind him to mitigate her sorrow. *Ambrose.*

[3] As if there is nothing dearer than an only son, so that grief upon the account of his death must be the greatest of all. *Carth. on the place.*

4. And yet, to heighten the affliction, it is further added, 'And she was a widow.' So that the staff of her age, on which she leaned, was broken:[1] she had now none left to comfort or assist her in her helpless, comfortless, state of widowhood; which is a condition not only void of comfort, but exposed to oppression and contempt.

Yea, and being a widow, the whole burden lay upon her alone; she had not a husband to comfort her, as Elkanah did Hannah (*1 Sam.* 1:8): 'Why weepest you, and why is your heart grieved? Am not I better to you than ten sons?' This would have been a great relief; but her husband was dead, as well as her son, both gone, and she only surviving to lament the loss of those comforts that once she had. Her calamities came not singly but one after another, and this reviving and aggravating the former. This was her case and condition when the Lord met her.

The Counsel of Christ

Secondly, Let us consider the counsel which Christ gave her, with respect to this her sad and sorrowful case. 'And when the Lord saw her, he had compassion on her, and said unto her, Weep not.' Relieving and supporting words; wherein we shall consider,

       1. The occasion

       2. The motive

       3. The counsel itself

---

[1] He was most dear to her on a twofold account, both because he was her only son, and that he was the comfort and support of her widowhood. *Piscator on the place.*

1. The *occasion* of it, and that was his seeing of her. This meeting at the gate of the city, how accidental and occasional soever it seems, yet without doubt it was providentially suited to the work intended to be wrought. The eye of his omniscience foresaw her, and this meeting was by him designed as an occasion of that famous miracle which he wrought upon the young man. Christ has a quick eye to discern poor, mourning, and disconsolate creatures; and though he be now in heaven, and stands out of our sight so that we see him not, yet he sees us, and his eye (which is upon all our troubles) still affects his heart and moves him to be compassionate towards us.

2. The *motive* stirring him up to give this relieving and comfortable counsel to her was his own compassion; she neither expected nor desired it from him; but so full of tender pity was the Lord towards her, that he goes before her with unexpected consolation. Her heart was nothing so full of compassion for her son as Christ was for her; he bore our infirmities, even natural as well as moral ones, in the days of his flesh; and though he be now exalted to the highest glory, yet still he continues as merciful as ever and as apt to be touched with the sense of our miseries (*Heb.* 4:15).

3. Consider the *counsel* itself, *Weep not;* herein fulfilling the office of comforter to them that mourn, whereunto he was anointed (*Isa.* 61:1–3). Yet the words are not an absolute prohibition of tears and sorrow; he does not condemn all mourning as sinful, or all expressions of grief for dead relations as uncomely; no, Christ would

not have his people stupid and without feeling; he only prohibits the excesses and extravagancies of our sorrows for the dead, that it should not be such a mourning for the dead as is found among the heathen, who sorrow without measure, because without hope, being ignorant of that grand relief which the gospel reveals.

The resurrection of her son from the dead is the ground upon which Christ builds her consolation and relief. Well might he say, 'Weep not', when he intended quickly to remove the cause of her tears, by restoring him again to life.

Now though there be somewhat in this case extraordinary and peculiar, for few or none that carry their dead children to the grave may expect to receive them again from the dead immediately by a special resurrection, as she did. I say, this is not to be expected by any that now lose their relations, the occasion and reason of such miraculous, special resurrections being removed by a sufficient and full evidence and confirmation of Christ's divine power and Godhead; yet those who now bury their relations, if they be such as die in Christ, have as good and sufficient reason to moderate their passions as this mourner had, and do as truly come within the reach and compass of his comfortable and supporting counsel, 'Weep not', as she did; for do but consider, what support or comfort can a particular and present resurrection from the dead give us more than that it is, and as it is, a specimen, handsel,[1] or pledge, of the general resurrection? It is

---

[1] That is, inaugural gift, often given at the start of a new year.

not the returning of the soul to its body, to live an animal life again in this world of sin and sorrow, and shortly after to undergo the agonies and pains of death again, that is in itself any such privilege as may afford much comfort to the person raised or his relations. It is no privilege to the person raised, for it returns him from rest to trouble, from the harbour back again into the ocean. It is a matter of trouble to many dying saints to hear of the likelihood of their returning again when they are got so nigh to heaven.

It was once the case of a godly minister of this nation who was much troubled at his return and said, 'I am like a sheep driven out of the storm almost to the fold, and then driven back into the storm again; or a weary traveller that is come near his home, and then must go back to fetch somewhat he had forgotten; or an apprentice, whose time is almost expired, and then must begin a new term.'

But to die, and then return again from the dead, has less of privilege than to return only from the brink of the grave; for the sick has not yet felt the agonies and last struggles or pangs of death; but such have felt them once and must feel them again – they must die twice, before they can be happy once; and besides, during the little time they spend on earth, between the first and second dissolution, there is a perfect $\alpha\mu\nu\eta\sigma\iota\alpha$ (amnesia), forgetfulness, and insensibleness, of all that which they saw or enjoyed in their state of separation; it being necessary both for them and others that it should be so. For themselves it is necessary, that they may be content to live and endure the time of separation from that blessed and ineffable state quietly and patiently;[1] and for others, that they may live by faith, and not by sense, and build upon divine, and not human authority and report.

So that here you see their agonies and pangs are doubled, and yet their lives not sweetened by any sense of their happiness which returns and remains with them; and therefore it can be no such privilege to them.

And as for their relations, though it may be some comfort to receive them again from the dead, yet the consideration that they are returned to them in the stormy sea, to partake of new sorrows and troubles from which they were lately free, and that in a short time they must part with them again, and feel the double sorrows of a parting pull which others feel but once; surely such a particular resurrection, considered in itself, is no such ground of comfort as at first we might imagine it to be.

It remains, then, that the ground of all solid comfort and relief against the death of our relations lies in the general and last resurrection, and what is in a particular one is but, as it were, a specimen[2] and evidence of the general; and there the apostle places our relief (*1 Thess.* 4:17), that we shall see and enjoy them again at the Lord's coming. And surely this is more than if (with this mother in the text) we should presently receive them from the dead as

---

[1] *Victurosque dii celant, ut vivere durent.*

  How long or short men live is kept a mystery,
  To make us both live well and less afraid to die.

[2] Therein we have a noble specimen of the future resurrection. *Calvin on the place.*

she did her son; and if we judge not so, it is because our hearts are carnal, and measure things rather by time and sense than by faith and eternity.

Thus you see the counsel, with its ground, which, for the most part, is common to other Christian mourners with her; the difference being but inconsiderable and of little advantage.

Here then, you find many aggravations of sorrow meeting together; a son, an only son, is carried to the grave; yet Christ commands the pensive mother not to mourn.

Hence we note —

DOCTRINE: *That Christians ought to moderate their sorrows for their dead relations, no matter how many afflicting circumstances and aggravations meet together in their death.*

2

Moderate and
Immoderate Sorrow

*I*t is as common with men, yea, with good men, to
exceed in their sorrows for dead relations[1] as it is to
exceed in their love and delights to living relations;
and both of the one and the other we may say, as they say
of waters, it is hard to confine them within their bounds.
It is therefore grave advice which the apostle delivers in
this case, 'But this I say, brethren, the time is short; it
remains that both they that have wives be as though they
had none; and they that weep, as though they wept not;
and they that rejoice, as though they rejoiced not' (*1 Cor.*
7:29, 30). As if he had said, the floating world is near its
port;[2] God has contracted the sails of man's life; it is but
a point of time we have to live, and shortly it will not be
a point to choose whether we had wives or not, children
or not. All these are time-eaten things, and before the
expected fruit of these comforts be ripe, we ourselves

[1] Whatever we love ardently while we have it, we lament bitterly when we
lose it. *Gregory on Job.*

[2] Καιρος συνεσταλμενος, that is, the time is contracted.

may be rotten. It is therefore a high point of wisdom to look upon things which shortly will not be as if already they were not, and to behave ourselves in the loss of these carnal enjoyments as the natural man behaves himself in the use of spiritual ordinances; he hears as if he heard not, and we should weep as if we wept not; their affections are a little moved sometimes by spiritual things, but they never lay them so to heart as to be broken-hearted for the sin they hear of, or deeply affected with the glory revealed. We also ought to be sensible of the stroke of God upon our dear relations; but yet still we must weep as if we wept not; that is, we must keep due bounds and moderation in our sorrows and not be too deeply concerned for these dying, short-lived things.

To this purpose, the apostle exhorts in Hebrews 12:5: 'My son, despise not the chastening of the Lord, nor faint when you are rebuked of him.' These are two extremes, despising and fainting. When God is correcting, to say, I do not regard it, let God take all, if he will; if my estate must go, let it go; if my children die, let them die: this is to despise the Lord's chastening, and God cannot bear it that we should bear it thus lightly.

There is also another extreme, and that is fainting. If when goods are taken away, the heart be taken away, and when children die, then the spirit of the parent die also, this is fainting under the rod. 'You lament', says Seneca, 'your deceased friend; but I would not have you grieve beyond what is meet. That you should not grieve at all, I dare not require you; tears may be excused, if they do not exceed. Let your eyes, therefore, be neither wholly dry, nor let them overflow. Weep you may, but wail you must not.'

Happy man that still keeps the golden bridle of moderation upon his passions and affections, and still keeps the possession of himself, whatsoever he lose the possession of.

Now, the method in which I propose to proceed shall be:

1. To discover the signs of immoderate sorrow;
2. To dissuade from the sin of it;
3. To remove the pleas for it;
4. To propose the cure for it.

3

Sorrow Permitted to Christian Mourners

I shall give you the signs of immoderate sorrow, and show you when it exceeds its bounds and becomes sinful, even a sorrow to be sorrowed for; and for clearness' sake, I will first allow what may be allowed to the Christian mourner, and then you will the better discern wherein the excess and sinfulness of your sorrow lies.

And *first*, However much we censure and condemn immoderate sorrow, *yet the afflicted must be allowed an awakened and tender sense of the Lord's afflicting hand upon them*. It is no virtue to bear what we do not feel; yea, it is a most unbecoming temper not to tremble when God is smiting.

The Lord said to Moses, in the case of Miriam, 'If her father had but spit in her face, should she not be ashamed seven days?' (*Num.* 12:14). The face is the table and seat of beauty and honour; but when it is spit upon, it is made the sink of shame. Had her own father spit upon her face when she had displeased him, would she not have gone aside, as one ashamed of such a rebuke, and not have showed her face to him again in seven days? How much more should she take it to heart and be sensible of this rebuke of mine, who have filled her face with leprous spots, the signs of my displeasure against her! Surely God will be ashamed of those that are not ashamed when he rebukes them.

It is not magnanimity, but stupidity, to make light of God's corrections; and for this the afflicted are smartly taxed: 'You have stricken them, but they have not grieved' (*Jer.* 5:3). When God smote Job in his person, children, and estate, he arose and tore his clothes, and put dust upon his head, to show that he was not senseless and unaffected; and yet he blessed the afflicting God, which as plainly showed that he was not contumacious and unsubmissive.

Secondly, *We must allow the mourning, afflicted soul a due and comely expression of his grief and sorrow in his complaints both to God and men.*

It is much more becoming a Christian ingenuously to open his troubles than sullenly to smother them. There is no sin in complaining *to* God, but much wickedness in complaining *of* him. Griefs are eased by groans and heart-pressures relieved by utterance.

This was David's course and constant way, who was a man of afflictions: 'I poured out my complaint before him; I showed before him my trouble. When my spirit was overwhelmed within me, then you knew my path' (*Psa.* 142:2–3).

To whom should children go but to their father, to make their moan? Whence may they expect relief and comfort but from him? The 102nd Psalm is entitled, 'A Prayer of the afflicted, when he is overwhelmed, and pours out his complaint before the LORD.'

And happy were it if every afflicted soul would choose this way to express his sorrows. Did we complain more to God, he would complain less of us, and quickly abate the matters of our complaint. Oh, you cannot think how moving, how melting, how prevailing it is with God, when his poor, burdened, and afflicted people are in a day of distress and despondency, and when deep calls unto deep, and one wave drives on another, then for the oppressed soul, with humility, filial confidence, and faith, to turn itself to the Lord, and thus speak to him:

> Father, what shall I do? My soul is greatly bowed down by trouble; I am full to the brim; my vain heart has looked for relief this way and that way, but none comes; every door of comfort is shut up against me. You have multiplied my sorrows, and renewed my witnesses against me; comfort is removed from my outward, and peace from my inner, man; sharp afflictions without, and bitter reflections within. O Lord, I am oppressed, undertake for me. Fathers of the flesh pity their distressed children, when they complain to them; and will not you, O Lord, whose compassions as far exceed creature-compassions as the sea exceeds a drop? O my Father, pity me, support me, deliver me!

Oh how acceptable this is to God! How advantageous to the soul!

We may also make our complaint to men. So did Job: 'Have pity, have pity on me, O my friends; for the hand of God has touched me' (*Job* 19:21) And it is a mercy if we have any friends that are wise, faithful, and experienced: they are born for such a time as this (*Prov.* 17:17); but be they what they will, they cannot pity as God, nor relieve and succour as he; and often we may say with Job, 'As for me, is my complaint to men? and if it were so, why should not my spirit be troubled?' (*Job* 21:4). What great advantage can I get by these complaints? I may burden the heart of my friend; but how little does that ease my own! Yet the very opening of the heart to an experienced, tender Christian, is some relief, and the engaging his prayers is more. Thus far you moan safely; in all this there is no danger.

Thirdly, *The afflicted person may (ordinarily) accuse, judge, and condemn himself, for being the cause and procurer of his own troubles.* He may lawfully be discontented and vexed with himself for his own folly, when the iniquity of his heels compasses him about. And truly it is but seldom that any great affliction befalls a gracious person but he saw the need of such a rod before he felt it.

Has God smitten your child or friend and did you not foresee some sharp trial coming? Did not your fond, secure, carnal temper need such a scourge to awaken, quicken, and purge you? Or, if you did not foresee it, it is now your duty to search and examine yourselves. So the church, in her affliction, resolved, 'Let us search and try our ways' (*Lam.* 3:40). When God is smiting, we should be searching. Surely our iniquities will inquire after us if we will not inquire after them: yea, in the day of affliction, a gracious soul is inquisitive about nothing more than about the procuring and provoking cause of its troubles. 'Show me wherefore you contend with me?' (*Job* 10:2). Lord, what special corruption is it that this rod is sent to rebuke? What sinful neglect does it come to humble me for? Oh, discover it now to me, and recover me now from it.

And having found the root and cause of their troubles, ingenuous souls will shame themselves for it, and give glory to God by a humble submission and vindication of the equity of his proceedings: 'I have sinned, what shall I do unto you, O preserver of men?' (*Job* 7:20). He thinks it no shame freely to discover his sin unto God, and deeply to abase himself before him for his folly.

I remember a choice note that Mr Brightman[1] has in his Commentary upon the Song of Solomon. He says:

> Holy men, after their hearts are renewed by repentance, are not ashamed to remember and confess their slips and shameful falls, to the glory of God; for they account, that the glory which such confessions take from them is not lost, whilst it goes to his honour.

If his glory may rise out of our shame, how willing should we be to take such shame to us? Holy David was not ashamed to acknowledge, 'My wounds stink, and are corrupt, because of my foolishness' (*Psa.* 38:5). He is the wisest man that thus makes himself a fool before God.

[1] Thomas Brightman (1562–1607).

It is true, God may afflict from prerogative or for trial; but we may always see cause enough in ourselves, and it is safest to charge it upon our own folly.

Lastly, *The afflicted Christian may, in a humble, submissive manner, plead with God, and be earnest for the removal of his affliction.*

When affliction presses us above strength, when it disables us for duty, or when it gives advantage to temptation, then we may say with David, 'Remove your stroke away from me: I am consumed by the blow of your hand' (*Psa.* 39:10). Even our Lord Jesus Christ, in the day of his troubles, poured out his soul with strong cries and many tears, saying, 'Father, if you are willing, remove this cup from me' (*Luke* 22:42). Oppressed nature desires ease, and even our renewed nature desires freedom from those clogs and temptations, which hinder us in duty, or expose us to snares.

4

When Sorrow
Becomes Sinful

*T*hus far we may safely go; but sorrow then becomes sinful and excessive, when,

First, It causes us to slight and despise all our other mercies and enjoyments as small things, in comparison with what we have lost.

It often falls out that the setting of one comfort clouds and darkens all the rest. Our tears for our lost enjoyments so blind our eyes that we cannot see the many other mercies which yet remain; we take so much notice of what is gone that we take little or no notice of what is left. But this is very sinful, for it involves in it both *ignorance, ingratitude*, and great *provocation*.

It is a sin springing from *ignorance*. Did we know the desert of our sins, we should rather wonder to see one mercy left than that twenty are cut off. They that know they have forfeited every mercy should be thankful that they enjoy any, and patient when they lose any of their comforts.

If you knew God, even that sovereign Lord at whose disposal our comforts come and go, who can the next moment blast all that remain, and turn you into hell afterwards, you would prize the mercies he yet indulges you with at a higher value. Did you understand the fickle, vanishing nature of the creature, what a flower, what a bubble it is; oh how thankful would you be to find so many yet left in your possession!

Did you know the case of thousands, as good as you, yea, better than you, whose whole harvest of comfort in this world is but a handful to the gleanings of comforts you still enjoy, who in all their lives never were owners of such comfortable enjoyments as you now overlook, surely you would not act as you do.

Besides, what vile *ingratitude* is in this! What, are all your remaining mercies worth nothing? You have buried a child, a friend; well, but still you have a husband, a wife, other children; or if not, you have comfortable accommodations for yourselves, with health to enjoy them; or if not, yet have you the ordinances of God, it may be, an interest in Christ and in the covenant, pardon of sin, and hopes of glory. What, and yet sink at this rate, as if all your mercies, comforts, and hopes, even in both worlds, were buried in one grave! Must Ichabod be written upon your best mercies because mortality is written upon one? Fie, fie, what shameful ingratitude is here!

And really, friend, such a carriage as this under the rod is no small *provocation* to the Lord to go on in judgment, and make a full end of all that remains, so that affliction shall not rise up the second time. What if God, taking notice how little you regard the many undeserved favours you yet possess, should say, Well, if you think them not worth the owning, neither do I think them worth the continuing? Go, death; there is a husband, a wife, other children yet left, smite them all. Go, sickness, and remove the health of his body yet left; go losses, and impoverish his estate yet left; go, reproach, and blast his reputation, which is yet sweet; what would you think of this? And yet, if you be out of Christ, you are in danger of a far sadder stroke than any, or all, yet mentioned. What if God should say, Do you not prize my mercy? Have you no value for my goodness and forbearance towards you? Is it nothing that I have spared you thus long in your sins and rebellions? Well then, I will stretch out my hand upon your life, cut off that thread which has kept you so many years from dropping into hell.

Oh, think, then, what you have done by provoking the Lord, through your vile ingratitude! It is a dangerous thing to provoke God, when he is already in a way of judgment. And if you be his own people, and so out of the danger of this last and worst stroke, yet know you have better mercies to lose than any you have yet lost. Should God cloud your souls with doubts, let loose Satan to buffet you, remove joy and peace from your inner man, how soon would you be convinced that the funeral of your dearest friend is but a trifle to this!

Well then, whatever God takes, be still thankful for what he leaves. It was the great sin of Israel in the wilderness, that though God had delivered them from their cruel servitude in Egypt, miraculously fed them in the desert, and was leading them on to a land flowing with milk and honey, yet, as soon as any want did but begin to pinch them, presently all these mercies were forgotten and blighted. 'Would God', say they, 'that we had died in the land of Egypt' (*Num.* 14:2). 'There is nothing at all, beside this manna' (*Num.* 11:6). Beware of this, O mourning and afflicted ones. You see both the sin that is in it, and the danger that attends it.

Secondly, and no less sinful, are our sorrows *when they so wholly engulf our hearts that we either mind not at all, or are little or nothing sensible of, the public evils and calamities which lie upon the church and people of God.*

Some Christians have such public spirits that the church's troubles swallow up their personal troubles. Melanchthon seemed to take little notice of the death of his child which he dearly loved, being almost overwhelmed with the miseries lying on the church.

And it was a good evidence of the graciousness and public-mindedness of Eli's spirit, who, sitting in the gate anxiously waiting for tidings from the army, when the tidings came that Israel fled before the Philistines, that his two sons, Hophni and Phinehas were dead, and the ark of God was taken, just at the mention of that word, *The ark of God,*[1] before he heard out the whole narration, his

[1] 'When he made mention of the ark of God': that is, hearing, not the whole account but a part, his mind ran on ahead and, foreseeing the conclusion, he fell. *Meteoz., on the place.*

mind quickly presaged the issue, he sank down and died (*1 Sam.* 4:17–18). Oh, that was the sinking, the killing word; had the messenger stopped at the death of his two sons, like enough he had supported that burden; but the loss of the ark was more to him than sons or daughters.

But how few such public spirits appear, even among professors, in this selfish generation! May we not, with the apostle, complain, 'All seek their own, not the things which are Jesus Christ's' (*Phil.* 2:21)? Few men have any great cares or designs lying beyond the bounds of their own private interests. And what we say of cares is as true of sorrows: if a child die, we are ready to die too, but public calamities pierce us not.

How few suffer either their domestic comforts to be swallowed up in the church's troubles, or their domestic troubles to be swallowed up by the church's mercies! Now, when it is thus with us, when we little regard what mercies or miseries lie upon others, but are wholly intent upon our own afflictions, this is a sinful sorrow, and ought to be sorrowed for.

Thirdly, Our sorrows then become sinful and exorbitant *when they divert us from, or distract us in our duties, so that our intercourse with heaven is stopped and interrupted by them.*

How long can we sit alone musing upon a dead creature? Here our thoughts easily flow; but how hard to fix them upon the living God! When our hearts should be in heaven with our Christ, they are in the grave with our dead. May not many afflicted souls justly complain that their troubles had taken away their Christ from them (I mean as to sweet sensible communion), and laid the dead child in his room?

Poor creature, cease to weep any longer for your dead relation, and weep rather for your dead heart. Is this your compliance with God's design in afflicting you? What, to grow a greater stranger to him than before! Or is this the way to your cure and comfort in affliction, to refrain from prayer, and turn your back upon God?

Or if you dare not wholly neglect your duty, yet your affliction spoils the success and comfort of it; your heart is wandering, dead, distracted in prayer and meditation, so that you have no relief or comfort from it.

Rouse up yourself, Christian, and consider, this is not right. Surely the rod works not kindly now. What, did your love to God expire when your friend expired? Is your heart as cold in duty as his body is in the grave?

Has natural death seized him, and spiritual deadness seized you? Surely then you have more reason to lament your dead heart than your dead friend. Divert the stream of your troubles speedily, and labour to recover yourself out of this temper quickly, lest sad experience shortly tell you that what you now mourn for is but a trifle to what you shall mourn for hereafter. To lose the heavenly warmth and spiritual liveliness of your affections is undoubtedly a far more considerable loss than to lose the wife of your bosom, or the sweetest child that ever a tender parent laid in the grave.

Reader, if this be your case, you have reason to challenge the first place among the mourners. It is better for you to bury ten sons, than to remit one degree of love or delight in God. The end of God in smiting was to win your heart nearer to him, by removing that which estranged it; how then do you cross the very design of God in this dispensation? Must God then lose his delight in your fellowship, because you have lost yours in the creature? Surely, when your troubles thus accompany you to your closet, they are sinful and extravagant troubles.

Fourthly, Then you may also conclude your sorrows to be excessive and sinful *when they so overload and oppress your bodies as to endanger your lives, or render them useless and unfit for service.*

Worldly sorrow works death (2 *Cor.* 7:10), that is, sorrow after the manner of worldly men;[1] sorrow in a mere carnal, natural way, which is not relieved by any spiritual reasonings and considerations. This falls so heavily sometimes upon the body that it sinks under the weight, and is cast into such diseases as are never more wrought off or healed in this world. 'Heaviness in the heart of man makes it stoop', says Solomon (*Prov.* 12:25). The stoutest body must stoop under heart-pressures.

It is with the mind of a man, says one, as with the stone *tyrhenus;* as long as it is whole it swims; but once broken, it sinks presently. Grief is a moth which, getting into the

---

[1] Worldly sorrow is after the manner of the world, arising from the love of it. Estius [Willem van Est] on the place.

mind, will, in a short time, make the body, be it never so strong and well-wrought a piece, like an old threadbare garment.

Philosophers and physicians generally reckon sorrow among the chief causes of shortening life. Christ was a man of sorrows and acquainted with grief, and this, some think, was the reason that he appeared as a man of fifty, when he was little more than thirty years old (*John* 8:57). But his sorrows were of another kind.[1]

Many a man's soul is to his body as a sharp knife to a thin sheath, which easily cuts it through; and what do we by poring and pondering upon our troubles but whet the knife that it may cut the deeper and quicker? Of all the creatures that ever God made (devils only excepted), man is the most able and apt to be his own tormentor.

How unmercifully do we load our bodies in times of afflictions! How do we not only waste their strength by sorrow, but deny relief and necessary refreshment! They must carry the load, but be allowed no refreshment. If they can eat the bread of affliction and drink tears, they may feed to the full; but no pleasant bread, no quiet sleep is permitted them.

Surely you would not burden a beast as you do your own bodies. You would pity and relieve a brute beast, groaning and sinking under a heavy burden, but you will not pity nor relieve your own bodies. Some men's souls

---

[1] 'These things write I unto you, who have wept so immoderately, that I am become an example (which I always abhorred) of those whom grief has overcome. Yet this unreasonable conduct I now condemn myself for.' *Seneca, Epistle 63 (On Grief for Lost Friends).*

have given such deep wounds to their bodies that they are never like to enjoy many easy or comfortable days more whilst they dwell in them.

Now, this is very sinful and displeasing to God; for if he have such a tender care for our bodies that he would not have us swallowed up of over much grief, no, though it be for sin (2 *Cor.* 2:7), but even to that sorrow sets bounds, how much less with outward sorrow for temporal loss? May not your stock of natural strength be employed to better purposes, think you, than these? Time may come that you may earnestly wish you had that health and strength again to spend for God which you now so lavishly waste and prodigally cast away upon your troubles, to no purpose or advantage.

It was therefore a high point of wisdom in David, and recorded no doubt for our imitation, who when the child was dead ceased to mourn, arose, washed himself, and did eat bread (2 *Sam.* 12:20).

Fifthly, *When affliction sours the spirit with discontent, and makes it inwardly grudge against the hand of God, then our trouble is full of sin, and we ought to be humbled for it before the Lord.*

Whatever God does with us or ours, still we should maintain good thoughts of him. A gracious heart cleaves nearer and nearer to God in affliction, and can justify God in his severe strokes, acknowledging them to be all just and holy: 'I know, O LORD, that your judgments are right, and that you in faithfulness have afflicted me' (*Psa.* 119:75). And hereby the soul may comfortably evidence to itself its own uprightness and sincere love to God; yea, it has been of singular use to some souls, to take right measures of their love to God in such trials. To have lovely and well-pleased thoughts of God, even when he smites us in our nearest and dearest comforts, argues plainly that we love him for himself, and not for his gifts only. And thus his interest in the heart is deeper than any creature-interest is. And such is the comfort that has resulted to some from such discoveries of their own hearts by close smarting afflictions that they would not part with it to have their comforts (whose removal occasioned them) given back in lieu of it.

But to swell with secret discontent, and have hard thoughts of God, as if he had done us wrong, or dealt more severely with us than any: oh, this is a vile temper, cursed fruit springing from an evil root; a very carnal, ignorant, proud heart; or at least from a very distempered, if renewed, heart. So it was with Jonah, when God smote his gourd: 'Yea', says he, 'I do well to be angry, even unto death' (*Jon.* 4:9). Poor man, he was highly distempered at this time, and out of frame. This was not his true temper or ordinary frame but a surprise, the effect of a paroxysm of temptation, in which his passions had been over-heated.

Few dare to vent it in such language: but how many have their hearts embittered by discontent and secret risings against the Lord? Which, if ever the Lord open their eyes to see, will cost them more trouble, than ever that affliction did which gave the occasion of it.

I deny not but that the best heart may be tempted to think and speak frowardly concerning these works of the Lord; that envious adversary, the devil, will blow the coals, and labour to blow up our spirits at such times into high discontentment. The temptation was strong even upon David himself, to take up hard thoughts of God, and to conclude, 'Verily I have cleansed my heart in vain' (*Psa.* 73:13), that is, how little privilege from the worst of evils has a man by his godliness? But he soon suppressed such motions: 'If I . . . speak thus . . . I should offend against the generation of your children' (*Psa.* 73:15): meaning, that he should condemn the whole race of godly men through the whole world; for who is there among them all but is, or has been, or may be, afflicted as severely as myself?

'Surely it is meet to be said unto God, I have borne chastisement, I will not offend any more' (*Job* 34:31). Whatever God does with you, speak well and think well of him and his works.

Sixthly, Our sorrows exceed due bounds *when we continually excite and provoke them by willing irritations.*

Grief, like a lion, loves to play with us before it destroys us. And strange it is that we should find some kind of pleasure in rousing our sorrows. It is Seneca's observation,[1] and experimentally true, that even sorrow itself has

---

[1] Sorrow itself has a certain kind of pleasure attending it; when the parents call to mind the pleasant sayings, the cheerful conversation, and the filial affection of their children, then their eyes are refreshed as it were with a kind of joy (*Epistle* 99).

[31]

a certain kind of delight attending it. The Jews, who were with Mary in the house to comfort her, 'When they saw that she went out hastily, followed her, saying, She goes to the grave to weep there' (*John* 11:31); as they do, says Calvin, that seek to provoke their troubles, by going to the grave, or often looking upon the dead body.

Thus we delight to look upon the relics of our deceased friends, and often to mention their actions and sayings, not so much for any matter of holy and weighty instruction or imitation, for that would warrant, and commend the action; but rather to rub the wound, and fetch fresh blood from it, by piercing ourselves with some little, trivial, yet wounding, circumstances. I have known many that will sit and talk of the features, actions, and sayings of their children for hours together, and weep at the rehearsal of them, and that for many months after they are gone, so keeping the wound continually open, and excruciating their own hearts, without any benefit at all by them. A lock of hair, or some such trifles, must be kept for this purpose, to renew their sorrow daily, by looking on it. On this account, Jacob would not have his son called *Benoni*, the son of my sorrow, lest it should renew his sorrow, but *Benjamin*.

I am far from commending a brutish oblivion of our dear relations, and condemn it as much as I do this childish and unprofitable remembrance. O friends! we have other things to do under the rod than these. Were it not better to be searching our hearts, and houses, when God's rod is upon us, and studying how to answer the end of it, by mortifying those corruptions which provoke it? Surely the rod works not kindly till it comes to this.

Seventhly, Lastly, our sorrows may then be pronounced sinful *when they deafen our ears to all the wholesome and seasonable words of counsel and comfort offered us for our relief and support.*

'A voice was heard in Ramah, lamentation, and bitter weeping; Rachel weeping for her children refused to be comforted, because they were not' (*Jer.* 31:15). She will admit no comfort, her disease is curable by no other means but the restoration of her children; give her them again and she will be quiet, else you speak into the air; she regards not whatever you say.

Thus it was with Israel in their cruel bondage in Egypt. Moses brings them the glad tidings of deliverance, 'But they hearkened not unto [him], for anguish of spirit, and for cruel bondage' (*Exod.* 6:9).

Thus obstinately fixed are many in their trouble that no words of advice or comfort find any place with them; yea, I have known some exceedingly quick and ingenious, even above the rate of their common parts and abilities, in inventing shifts and framing objections to turn off comfort from themselves, as if they had been hired to plead against their own interest. And if they be driven from those pleas, yet they are settled in their troubles too fast to be moved. Say what you will, they mind it not, or, at most it abides not upon them. Let proper, seasonable advice or comfort be tendered, they refuse it; your counsel is good, but they have no heart to it now. Thus, 'My soul [says Asaph] refused to be comforted' (*Psa.* 77:2).

To want comfort in time of affliction is an aggravation of our affliction; but to refuse it when offered us wants not sin. The time may come when we would be glad to receive comfort or hear a word of support and shall be denied it.

Oh, it is a mercy to the afflicted to have Barnabas with them, an interpreter, one among a thousand; and it will be the great sin and folly of the afflicted to spill like water upon the ground those excellent cordials, prepared and offered to them, out of a froward or dead spirit under trouble. Say not with them in Lamentations 3:18–19, 'My hope is perished from the LORD: remembering mine affliction and my misery, the wormwood and the gall.' It is a thousand pities that the wormwood and gall of affliction should so disgust a Christian as that he should not at any time be able to relish the sweetness that is in Christ and in the promises.

And thus I have despatched the first part of my design, in showing you wherein the sin of mourners does not lie, and in what it does.

5

Counsel to Ungodly Mourners

*H*aving cleared this, and shown you wherein the sin and danger lie, my way is now prepared to the second thing proposed, namely, to dissuade mourners from these sinful excesses of sorrows, and keep the golden bridle of moderation upon their passions in times of affliction. And, oh, that my words may be as successful upon those pensive souls that shall read them as Abigail's were upon David, who, when he perceived how proper and seasonable they were, said, 'Blessed be the LORD God of Israel, which sent you this day to meet me: and blessed be your advice' (*1 Sam.* 25:32–33)!

I am sensible how hard a task it is that I here undertake, to charm down and allay mutinous, raging, and tumultuous passions. To give a check to the torrent of passion is ordinarily but to provoke it and make it rage and swell the more.

The work is the Lord's; it wholly depends upon his power and blessing. He that says to the sea when the waves thereof roar, 'Be still', can also quiet and compose the stormy and tumultuous sea that rages in the breasts of the afflicted, and casts up nothing but the froth of vain and useless complaints of our misery, or the dirt of sinful and wicked complaints against the dealings of the Lord with us.

The rod of affliction goes round and visits all sorts of persons, without difference; it is upon the tabernacles of the just and the unjust, the righteous and the wicked; both are mourning under the rod.

The godly are not so to be minded as that the other be wholly neglected; they have as strong and tender, though not as regular affections to their relations, and must not be wholly suffered to sink under their unrelieved burdens.

Here, therefore, I must have respect to two sorts of persons, whom I find in tears on the same account, I mean, the loss of their dear relations: the regenerate, and the unregenerate. I am a debtor to both, and shall aim at their support and assistance, for even the unregenerate call for our help and pity, and must not be neglected and wholly slighted in their afflictions. We must pity them who cannot pity themselves.[1] The law of God commands us to help a *beast*, if fallen under its burden; how much more a *man* sinking under a load of sorrows?

I confess, uses of comfort to the unregenerate are not (ordinarily) in use among us, and it may seem strange

---

[1] *Nihil miserius misero non miserante se ipsum*, that is, None is more to be pitied than a poor sinner that does not pity himself (Augustine).

whence any thing of support should be drawn for them that have no special interest in Christ or the promises.

I confess also that I find myself under great disadvantages for this work; I cannot offer them those reviving cordials which are contained in Christ and the covenant for God's afflicted people; but yet, such is the goodness of God, even to his enemies, that they are not left wholly without supports or means to allay their sorrow.

If this, therefore, be your case, who read these lines; afflicted and unsanctified, mourning bitterly for your dead friends, and more cause to mourn for your dead soul, Christless and graceless, as well as childless or friendless; no comfort in hand, nor yet in hope; full of trouble, and no vent by prayer or faith to ease your heart—Poor creature! Your case is sad; but yet do not wholly sink and suffer yourself to be swallowed up of grief: you have laid your dear one in the grave, yet throw not yourself headlong into the grave after him; that will not be the way to remedy your misery. But sit down awhile, and ponder these three things.

First, *That of all persons in the world, you have most reason to be tender over your life and health, and careful to preserve it, for if your troubles destroy you, you are eternally lost, undone for ever.* 'Worldly sorrow [says the apostle] works death.' And if it works your death, it works your damnation also; for hell follows that pale horse (*Rev.* 6:8). If a believer die, there is no danger of hell to him, the second death has no power over him; but woe to you if it overtake you in your sin. Beware, therefore, what you do against your health and life; do not put the candle of sorrow too near that thread by which you hang over the mouth of hell. Oh, it is far better to be childless or friendless on earth, than hopeless and remediless in hell.

Secondly, *Own and admire the bounty and goodness of God manifested to you in this affliction;* that when death came into your family to smite and carry off one, it had not fallen to your lot to be the person; your husband, wife, or child is taken, and you are left. Had your name been in the commission, you had been now past hope.

Oh, the sparing mercy of God! The wonderful long-suffering of God towards you! Possibly that poor creature that is gone never provoked God as you have done; your poor child never abused mercies, neglected calls, treasured up the ten thousandth part of guilt that you have done; so that you might well imagine that death should rather have cut you down that had so provoked God than your poor little one.

But oh, the admirable patience of God! Oh, the riches of his long-suffering! You are only warned, not smitten by it. Is there nothing in this worth thankful acknowledgment? Is it not better to be in black for another on earth than in the blackness of darkness for ever? Is it not easier to go to the grave with your dead friend, and weep there, than to go to hell among the damned, where there is weeping, and wailing, and gnashing of teeth?

Thirdly, *This affliction for which you mourn may be the greatest mercy to you that ever yet befell you in this world*. God has now made your heart soft by trouble, showed you the vanity of this world, and what a poor trifle it is which you made your happiness. There is now a dark cloud spread over all your worldly comforts. Now, oh, now! if the Lord would but strike in with this affliction, and by it open your eyes to see your deplorable state, and take off your heart for ever from the vain world, which you now see has nothing in it; and cause you to choose Christ, the only abiding good for your portion – if now your affliction may but bring your sin to your remembrance, and your dead friend may but bring you to a sense of your dead soul, which is as cold to God and spiritual things as his body is to you; and more loathsome in his eyes than that corpse is, or shortly will be to the eyes of men; then this day is certainly a day of the greatest mercy that ever yet you saw. O happy death, that shall prove life to your soul!

Why, this is sometimes the way of the Lord with men: 'If they are bound in fetters, and held in cords of affliction; then he shows them their work, and their transgressions that they have exceeded. He opens also their ear to discipline, and commands that they return from iniquity' (*Job* 36:8–9).

Oh consider, poor pensive creature, that which stole away your heart from God is now gone; that which ate up your time and thoughts, so that there was no room for God, soul, or eternity in them, is gone; all the vain expectations that you raised up to yourself from that poor creature which now lies in the dust are in one day quite perished. Oh, what an advantage you now have for heaven, beyond whatever you yet had! If God will but bless this rod, you will have cause to keep many a thanksgiving day for this day.

I pray, let these three things be pondered by you. I can bestow no more comforts upon you; your condition bars the best comforts from you; they belong to the people of God, and you have yet nothing to do with them.

I shall therefore turn from you to them, and present some choicer comforts to them, to whom they properly belong, which may be of great use to you in reading, if it be but to convince you of the blessed privilege and state of the people of God in the greatest plunges of troubles in this world, and what advantages their interest in Christ gives them for peace and settlement, beyond that state you are in.

6

Godly Mourners
Comforted

*A*nd here I do with much more freedom and hope of success apply myself to the work of counselling and comforting the afflicted. You are the fearers of the Lord, and tremble at his Word; the least sin is more formidable to you than the greatest affliction. Doubtless you would rather choose to bury all your children than provoke and grieve your heavenly Father. Your relations are dear, but Christ is dearer to you by far.

Well then, let me persuade you to retire awhile into your closets, redeem a little time from your unprofitable sorrows, ease and empty your hearts before the Lord, and beg his blessing upon the relieving, quieting, and heart-composing considerations that follow, some of which are more general and common, some more particular and special; but all of them such as, through the blessing of God, may be very useful at this time to your souls.

Consideration 1. Consider, in this day of sorrow, who is the framer and author of this rod by which you now smart; is it not the Lord? And if the Lord has done it, it becomes you meekly to submit. 'Be still, and know that I am God' (*Psa.* 46:10).

Man and man stand on even ground. If your fellow-creature does any thing that displeases you, you may not only inquire who did it, but why he did it? You may demand his grounds and reasons for what he has done; but you may not do so here. It is expected that this one thing, *The Lord has done it,* should, without any further disputes or contests, silence and quiet you, whatever it be that he has done. 'Why do you strive against him? for he gives not account of any of his matters' (*Job* 33:13). The Supreme Being must needs be an unaccountable and uncontrollable Being.

It is a shame for a child to strive with his father; a shame for a servant to contend with his master; but for a creature to quarrel and strive with the God that made him, oh how shameful it is! Surely it is highly reasonable that you be subject to that will whence you proceeded, and that he who formed you and yours should dispose of both as seems him good. It is said in 2 Samuel 3:36, that 'whatsoever the king did pleased all the people'; and shall any thing the Lord does displease you? He can do no wrong. If we pluck a rose in the bud as we walk in our gardens, who shall blame us for it? It is our own, and we can crop it off when we please. Is not this your case? Your sweet bud, which was cropped off before it was fully blown, was cropped off by him that owned it, yea, by him that formed it.

If his dominion be absolute, sure his disposal should be acceptable. It was so to good Eli, 'It is the LORD: let him do what seems him good' (*1 Sam*. 3:18); and it was so to David, 'I was dumb, I opened not my mouth; because you did it' (*Psa*. 39:9). Oh, let it be for ever remembered that he 'whose name alone is JEHOVAH, is the Most High over all the earth' (*Psa*. 83:18).

The glorious sovereignty of God is illustriously displayed in two things, his decrees and his providences. With respect to the first, he says, 'I will have mercy on whom I will have mercy' (*Rom*. 9:15). Here is no ground of disputing with him; for 'O man, who are you that reply against God? Shall the thing formed say to him that formed it, Why have you made me thus? Has not the potter power over the clay?'

And as to his providences, wherein his sovereignty is also manifested, it is said in Zechariah 2:13, 'Be silent, O all flesh, before the LORD: for he is raised up out of his holy habitation.' It is spoken of his providential working in the changes of kingdoms, and the desolations that attend them.

Now, seeing the case stands thus, that the Lord has done it, that it is his pleasure to have it so, and that if it had not been his will, it could never have been as it is; he that gave you (or rather lent you) your relation, has also taken him: Oh, how quiet should this consideration leave you! If your landlord, who has many years suffered you to dwell in his house, does at last warn you out of it, though he tells you not why, you will not contend with him, or say he has done you wrong; much less if he tells you it will be more for his profit and accommodation to take it into his own hand than let it to you any longer.

Doubtless, reason will tell you that you ought quietly to pack up and leave it. It is your great landlord, from whom you hold (at pleasure) your own and your relations' lives, that has now warned you out from one of them, it being more for his glory, it may be, to take it in his own hands by death; and must you dispute the case with him?

Come, Christian, this no way becomes you; but rather, 'The Lord gave, and the Lord has taken away; blessed be the name of the Lord' (*Job* 1:21). Look off from a dead creature; lift up your eyes to the sovereign, wise, and holy pleasure that ordered this affliction. Consider who he is, and what you are; yea, pursue this consideration, till you can say, I am now filled with the will of God.

Consideration 2. Ponder well the quality of the comfort you are deprived of, and remember that, when you had it, it stood but in the rank and order of common and inferior comforts.

Children, and all other relations, are but common blessings, which God bestows indifferently upon his friends and enemies, and by the having or losing of them, no man knows either love or hatred. It is said of the wicked in Psalm 17:14 that they are full of children; yea, and of children that do survive them too; for *they leave their substance to their babes.* Full of sin, yet full of children, and these children live to inherit their parents' sins and estates together. It is mistaking the quality and nature of our enjoyments that so plunges us into trouble when we lose them. We think there is so necessary a connection between these creatures and our happiness that we are utterly undone when they fail us. But this is our mistake. There is no such necessary connection or dependence. We may be happy without these things. It is not father, mother, wife, or child in which our chief good and felicity lie; we have higher, better, and more enduring things than these; all these may perish, and yet our souls be secure and safe; yea, and our comfort in the way, as well as in the end, may be safe enough, though these are gone. God has better things to comfort his people with than these, and worse rods to afflict you with than the removal of these. Had God let your children live and flourish, and given you ease and rest in your tabernacle, but in the mean time inflicted spiritual judgments upon your souls, how much more sad had your case been!

But as long as our best mercies are all safe, the things that have salvation in them remain, and only the things that have vanity in them are removed, you are not prejudiced or much hindered as to the attainment of your last end by the loss of these things.

Alas! it was not Christ's intent to purchase for you a sensual content in the enjoyment of these earthly comforts, but to redeem you from all iniquity, purge your corruptions, sanctify your natures, wean your hearts from this vain world, and so to dispose and order your present condition that, finding no rest and content here, you might the more ardently pant and sigh after the rest which remains for the people of God. And are you not in as probable a way to attain this end now as you were before? Do you think you are not as likely, by these methods of providence, to be weaned from the world, as by more pleasant and prosperous ones? Every wise man reckons that station and condition to be best for him which most promotes and secures his last end and great design.

Well then, reckon that you are as well without these things as with them; yea, and better too, if they were but clogs and snares upon your affections; you have really lost nothing if the things wherein your eternal happiness consists be yet safe. Many of God's dearest children have been denied such comforts as these, and many have been deprived of them, and yet they were never the farther from Christ and heaven for that.

Consideration 3. Always remember that, however soon and unexpected your parting with your relations was, yet your lease was expired before you lost them, and you enjoyed them every moment of the time that God intended them for you.

Before this relation whose loss you lament was born, the time of your enjoyment and separation was unalterably fixed and limited in heaven by the God of the spirits of all flesh; and although it was a secret to you whilst your friend was with you, yet now it is a plain and evident thing that this was the time of separation before appointed; and that the life of your friend could by no means be protracted or abbreviated, but must keep you company just so far, and then part with you.

This position lacks no full and clear Scripture authority for its foundation. How pregnant and full is that text in Job 14:5, 'Seeing his days are determined, the number of his months are with you, you have appointed him his bounds that he cannot pass.'

The time of our life, as well as the place of our habitation, was fixed before we were born.

It will greatly conduce to your settlement and peace to be well established in this truth – that the appointed time was fully come when you and your dear relation parted – for it will prevent and save a great deal of trouble, which comes from our after-reflections.

Oh, if this had been done, or that omitted; had it not been for such miscarriages and oversights, my dear husband, wife, or child, had been alive at this day! No, no, the Lord's time was fully come, and all things concurred, and fell in together to bring about the pleasure of his will. Let that satisfy you: had the ablest physicians in the world been there, or had they that were there prescribed another course, as it is now so it would have been when they had done all. Only it must be precautioned that the decree of God no way excuses any voluntary or sinful neglects or miscarriages. God over-rules these things to serve his own ends, but no way approves them. But it greatly relieves against all our involuntary and unavoidable oversights and mistakes about the use of means or the timing of them that it could not be otherwise than now it is.

Objection. But many things are alleged against this position, and that with much seeming countenance from such scriptures as these: 'Bloody and deceitful men shall not live out half their days' (*Psa.* 55:23); 'Why should you die before your time?' (*Eccles.* 7:17); 'O my God, take me not away in the midst of my days' (*Psa.* 102:24); 'I am deprived of the residue of my years' (*Isa.* 38:10); 'The fear of the LORD prolongs days: but the years of the wicked shall be shortened' (*Prov.* 10:27). It is demanded, what tolerable sense we can give to these Scriptures, whilst we assert an unalterable fixing of the term of death?

Solution. The sense of all these scriptures will be cleared up to our full satisfaction by distinguishing death and the terms of it.

First, We must distinguish death into *natural* and *violent.* The wicked and blood-thirsty man shall not live out half his days, that is, half so long as he might live according to the course of nature, or the vigour and soundness of his natural constitution; for his wickedness either drowns nature in an excess of riot and luxury or exposes him to the hand of justice, which cuts him off for his wickedness before he has accomplished half his days.

Again, we must distinguish the term or limit for death, which is either *general* or *special.*

The *general* limits are now seventy or eighty years: 'The days of our years are threescore years and ten; and if by reason of strength they be fourscore years, yet is their strength labour and sorrow' (*Psa.* 90:10). To this short limit the life of man is generally reduced since the flood; and though there are some few exceptions, yet the general rule is not thereby destroyed.

The *special* limit is that proportion of time which God by his own counsel and will has allotted to every individual person; and it is only known to us by the event: this we affirm to be a fixed and immovable term; with it all things shall fall in and observe the will of God in our dissolution at that time.

But because the general limit is known, and the special limit is a secret hid in God's own breast, therefore man reckons by the former account, and may be said, when he dies at thirty or forty years old, to be cut off in the midst of his days; for it is so, reckoning by the general account, though he be not cut off till the end of his days, reckoning by the special limit.

Thus he that is wicked dies before his time, the time that he might attain to in an ordinary way; but not before the time God has appointed; and the case is the same in all the other objected scriptures.

It is not proper at all in a subject of this nature to digress into a controversy. Alas! the poor mourner, overwhelmed with grief, has no pleasure in that; it is not proper for him at this time, and therefore I shall, for the present, waive the controversy and wind up this consideration with a humble and serious motion to the afflicted that they will wisely consider the matter. The Lord's time was come;

your relations lived with you every moment that God intended them for you before you had them.

O parents! mind this, I beseech you; the time of your child's continuance in the womb was fixed to a minute by the Lord; and when the parturient[1] fullness of that time was come, were you not willing that it should be delivered thence into the world? The tender mother would not have it abide one minute longer in the womb, however well she loved it; and is there not the same reason we should be willing, when God's appointed time is come, to have it delivered by death out of this state which, in respect of the life of heaven, is but as the life of a child in the womb to its life in the open world.

And let none say the death of children is a premature death. God has ways to ripen them for heaven whom he intends to gather there eventually, which we know not. In respect of fitness they die in a full age, though they be cut off in the bud of their time.

He who appointed the seasons of the year appointed the seasons of our comfort in our relations; and as those seasons cannot be altered, no more can these. All the course of providence is guided by an unalterable decree; what falls out casually to our apprehension yet falls out necessarily in respect of God's appointment. Oh, therefore be quieted in it. This must needs be as it is.

Consideration 4. Has God smitten your darling, and taken away the delight of your eyes with this stroke? Bear this stroke with patience and quiet submission: for

[1] That is, bringing forth, or about to bring forth.

how do you know but your trouble might have been greater from the life than it now is from the death of your children?

Sad experience made a holy man once say, It is better to weep for ten dead children than for one living child. A living child may prove a continual dropping, yea, a continual dying to the parent's heart. What a sad word was that of David to Abishai, 'Behold' [says he], my son, which came forth of my bowels, seeks my life' (2 *Sam.* 16:11). I remember Seneca, in his consolatory epistle to his friend Marullus, brings in his friend thus aggravating the death of his child:

> Oh [says Marullus], had my child lived with me, to how great modesty, gravity, and prudence, might my discipline have formed and moulded him? But [says Seneca], (which is more to be feared), he might have been as most others are; for look [says he], what children come even out of the worthiest families; such as exercise both their own, and others' lusts; in all whose life there is not a day without the mark of some notorious wickedness upon it.[1]

I know that your tender love to your children will scarcely admit such jealousies of them; they were sweet, lovely, innocent companions, and you doubt not but by your care of their education and prayer for them they might have been the joy of your hearts.

Why, doubtless, Esau, when he was little, and in his tender age, promised as much comfort to his parents as Jacob did; and I question not but Isaac and Rebecca

[1] Seneca: *Epistle 99*.

(a glorious pair), spent as many prayers, and bestowed as many holy counsels upon him as they did upon his brother; but when the child grew up to riper years, then he became a sharp affliction to his parents; for it is said, that 'Esau was forty years old when he took to wife Judith, the daughter of Beeri the Hittite . . . which [was] a grief of mind to Isaac and Rebecca' (*Gen.* 26:34). The word rendered 'grief' comes from a root that signifies *to embitter*. This child embittered the minds of his parents by his rebellion against them and despising their counsels.

And I cannot doubt but that Abraham disciplined his family as strictly as any of you; never man received a higher encomium from God upon that account: 'I know him, that he will command his children and his household after him, and they shall keep the way of the LORD' (*Gen.* 18:19). Nor can I think but that he bestowed as many and as frequent prayers for his children, and particularly for his son Ishmael, as any of you. We find one, and that a very pitiful one, recorded in Genesis 17:18, 'O that Ishmael might live before you!' And yet you know how he proved a son that yielded him no more comfort than Esau did to Isaac and Rebecca.

Oh, how much more common it is for parents to see the vices and evils of their children than their virtues and graces! And where one parent lives to rejoice in beholding the grace of God shining forth in the life of his child, there are twenty, it may be a hundred, that live to behold, to their vexation and grief, the workings of corruption in them.

It is noted by Plutarch in his *Morals*[1] that Neocles lived not to see the noble victory obtained by Themistocles his son; nor Miltiades, to see the battle his son Cimon won in the field; nor Xanthippus, to hear his son Pericles preach and make orations. Ariston never heard his son Plato's lectures and disputations; but men (says he) commonly live to see their children fall a-gaming, revelling, drinking, and whoring: multitudes live to see such things to their sorrow. And if you be a gracious soul, oh what a cut would this be to your very heart! To see those (as David spoke of his Absalom) that came out of your bowels to be sinning against God, that God whom you love, and whose honour is dearer to you than your very life!

But admit that they should prove civil and hopeful children, yet might you not live to see more misery come upon them than you could endure to see? Oh, think what a sad and doleful sight was that to Zedekiah, 'The king of Babylon slew [his sons] before his eyes' (*Jer.* 52:10). Horrid spectacle!

Consideration 5. How know you but that by this stroke which you so lament God has taken them away from the evil to come?

It is God's usual way when some extraordinary calamities are coming upon the world to hide some of his weak and tender ones out of the way by death (*Isa.* 57:1–2). He leaves some and removes others; but takes care for the security of all. He provided a grave for Methuselah

---

[1] Plutarch: *Moralia (De Amore Prolis).*

before the flood. The grave is a hiding-place to some, and God sees it better for them to be underground than above ground in such evil days.

Just as a careful and tender father who has a son abroad at school, hearing the plague is broken out in or near the place, sends his horse presently to fetch home his son before the danger and difficulty be greater: so death is our Father's pale horse which he sends to fetch home his tender children and carry them out of harm's way.

Surely, when national calamities are drawing on, it is far better for our friends to be in the grave in peace than exposed to the miseries and distresses which are here, which is the meaning of Jeremiah 22:10, 'Weep not for the dead, neither bemoan him: but weep for him that goes away: for he shall return no more, nor see his native country.' And is there not a dreadful sound of troubles now in our ears? Do not the clouds gather blackness? Surely all things round about us seem to be preparing and disposing themselves for affliction. The days may be nigh, in which you shall say, 'Blessed is the womb that never bare, and the paps that never gave suck.'

It was in the day wherein the faith and patience of the saints were exercised that John heard a voice from heaven saying to him, 'Write, blessed are the dead which die in the Lord from henceforth.'

Your friend, by an act of favour, is disbanded by death, whilst you yourself are left to endure a great fight of affliction. And now, if troubles come, your cares and fears will be so much the less, and your own death so much the easier to you when so much of you is in heaven already. In this case, the Lord, by a merciful dispensation, is providing both for their safety and your own easier passage to them.

In removing your friends beforehand, he seems to say to you, as he did to Peter, 'What I do you know not now, but you shall know hereafter' (*John* 13:7). The eye of providence has a prospect far beyond yours; probably it would be a harder task for you to leave them behind than to follow them.

A tree that is deeply rooted in the earth, requires many strokes to fell it; but when its roots are loosened beforehand, then an easy stroke lays it down upon the earth.

Consideration 6. A parting time must needs come; and why is not this as good as another? You knew beforehand your child or friend was mortal, and the thread which linked you together must be cut. If any one (says Basil) had asked you, when your child was born, What is that which is born? what would you have answered? Would you not have said, It is a man? And if a man, then a mortal, vanishing thing. And why then are you surprised with wonder to see a dying thing dead?

He (says Seneca)[1] who complains that one is dead, complains that he was a man. All men are under the same condition: to whose share it falls to be born, to him it remains to die.

---

[1] Bear the law of necessity with an even mind . . . How many besides you must sorrow? *Seneca: Epistle 99.*

We are indeed distinguished by the intervals, but equalized in the issue: 'It is appointed unto men once to die' (*Heb.* 9:27). There is a statute law of heaven in the case.

Possibly you think this is the worst time for parting that could be. Had you enjoyed it longer, you could have parted easier. But how deceived you are in that! The longer you had enjoyed it, the more loath still you would have been to leave it; the deeper it would have rooted itself in your affections.

Had God given you such a privilege as was once granted to the English Parliament, that the union between you and your friend should not be dissolved till you yourself were willing it should be dissolved, when, think you, would you have been willing it should be dissolved?

It is well for us and ours that our times are in God's hand, and not in our own. And however immature your blessing seemed to be when it was cut down, yet it 'came to the grave in a full age, as a shock of corn in its season' (*Job* 5:26). They that are in Christ, and in the covenant, never die unseasonably, whenever they die, says one upon the text.

> They die in a good old age; yea, though they die in the spring and flower of youth; they die in a good old age; i.e., they are ripe for death whenever they die. Whenever the godly die, it is harvest time with him; though in a natural capacity he be cut down while he is green, and cropped in the bud or blossom; yet in his spiritual capacity he never dies before he is ripe; God can ripen him speedily,

he can let out such warm rays and beams of his Holy Spirit upon him, as shall soon mature the seeds of grace into a preparedness for glory.[1]

It was, doubtless the most fit and seasonable time for them that ever they could die in, and as it is a fit time for them, so for you also. Had your child lived longer, it might either have engaged you more, and so your parting would have been harder; or else have puzzled and stumbled you more, by discovering its natural corruption; and then, what a stinging aggravation of your sorrow would that have been!

Surely the Lord of time is the best judge of time; and in nothing do we more discover our folly and rashness, than in presuming to fix the times either of our comforts or our troubles. As for our comforts, we never think they can come too soon; we would have them presently, whether the season be fit or not, as Numbers 12:13, 'Heal her now, O God'; Oh, let it be done speedily. We are in post-haste for our comforts, but as for our afflictions, we never think they come late enough; not at this time, Lord; rather at any other time than now.

But it is good to leave the timing both of the one and the other to him, whose works are all beautiful in their seasons, and who never does any thing in an improper time.

Consideration 7. Call to mind in this day of trouble, the covenant you have with God, and what you solemnly promised him in the day you took him for your God.

[1] Joseph Caryl on Job 5:26.

It will be very seasonable and useful for you, Christian, at this time, to reflect upon these transactions, and the frame of your heart in those days, when a heavier load of sorrow pressed your heart than you now feel.

In your spiritual distresses, when the burden of sin lay heavy, the curse of the law, the fear of hell, the dread of death and eternity beset you on every side and shut you up to Christ, the only door of hope; ah! what good news would you then have accounted it, to escape that danger, with the loss of all earthly comforts! Was not this your cry in those days?

> Lord, give me Christ, and deny me whatever else you please! Pardon my sin, save my soul, and, in order to both, unite me to Christ, and I will never repine or open my mouth. Do what you will with me; let me be friendless, let me be childless, let me be poor, let me be any thing, rather than a Christless, graceless, hopeless soul.

And when the Lord hearkened to your cry, and showed you mercy; when he drew you off from the world into your closet, and there treated with you in secret, when he was working up your heart to the terms of his covenant, and made you willing to accept of Christ upon his own terms; oh then, how heartily did you submit to his yoke, as most reasonable and easy, as at that time it seemed to be to you!

Call to mind these days, the secret places where Christ and you made the bargain; have not these words, or words to this sense, been whispered by you into his ear, with a dropping eye and melting heart?

Lord Jesus, here am I, a poor guilty sinner, deeply laden with sin; fear and trouble upon one hand, and there is a just God, a severe law, and everlasting burnings, on the other hand; but blessed be God, O blessed be God for Jesus the Mediator, who interposes between me and it. You are the only door of hope at which I can escape, your blood the only means of my pardon and salvation. You have said, 'Come unto me all you that labour and are heavy laden.' You have promised, that he that comes to you shall in no wise be cast out.

Blessed Jesus, your poor creature comes to you upon these encouragements: I come; Oh, but it is with many staggerings, with many doubts and fears of the issue; yet I am willing to come and make a covenant with you this day.

I take you this day to be my Lord, and submit heartily to all your disposals; do what you will with me or mine, let me be rich or poor, anything, or nothing in this world; I am willing to be as you would have me, and I do likewise give myself to you this day to be yours; all I am, all I have shall be yours, yours to serve you, and yours to be disposed of at your pleasure. You shall henceforth be my highest Lord, my chiefest good, my last end.

Now, Christian, make good to Christ what you did so solemnly promise him. He, I say, *he* has disposed of this your dear relation, as pleased him, and is thereby trying your uprightness in the covenant which you made with him. Now where is the satisfaction and content you promised to take in all his disposals? Where is that covenanted submission to his will? Did you except this affliction that is come upon you?

Did you tell him, Lord, I will be content you shall, when you please, take any thing I have, save only this husband, this wife, or this dear child; I reserve this out of the bargain? I shall never endure that you should kill this comfort? If so, you did in all this but prove yourself a hypocrite; if you were sincere in your covenant, as Christ had no reserve on his part, so you had none on yours.

It was all without any exception you then resigned to him, and now will you go back from your word, as one that had out-promised himself, and repents the bargain? Or, at least, as one that has forgotten these solemn trans-actions in the days of your distress? Wherein has Christ failed in one tittle that he promised you? Charge him, if you can, with the least unfaithfulness; he has been faithful to a tittle on his part; oh, make sure your are so on yours; this day it is put to the proof. Remember what you have promised him.

Consideration 8. But if your covenant with God will not quiet you, yet I think God's covenant with you might be presumed to do it.

Is your family, which was lately hopeful and flourish-ing, a peaceful tabernacle, now broken up and scattered? Your posterity, from whom you raised up to yourself great expectations of comfort in old age, cut off, so that you are now likely neither to have a name or a memorial left you in the earth?

Do you sit alone, and mourn to think what have be-come of your hopes and comforts now?

Do you read over these words of Job, chapter 29:1–5, and comment upon them with many tears?

> Oh that I were as in months past, as in the day when God preserved me; when his candle shined upon my head, and when by his light I walked through darkness; as I was in the days of my youth, when the secret of God was upon my tabernacle; when the Almighty was yet with me, when my children were about me.

Yet let the covenant God has made with you comfort you in this your desolate condition.

You know what domestic troubles holy David met with in a sad succession, not only from the death of children, but, which was much worse, from the wicked lives of his children. There were incest, murder, and rebellion in his family; a far sorer trial than death in their infancy could have been; and yet, see how sweetly he relieves himself from the covenant of grace:

> Although my house be not so with God, yet he has made with me an everlasting covenant, ordered in all things, and sure, for this is all my salvation and all my desire, although he make it not to grow.

I know that this place principally refers to Christ, who was to spring out of David's family, according to God's covenant made with him in that behalf; and yet I doubt not but that it has another, though less principal aspect to his own family, over all the afflictions and troubles where-of the covenant of God with him did abundantly comfort him. And as it comforted him, although his house did not increase, and those that were left were not such as he desired, so it may abundantly comfort you also, whatever troubles, or deaths, are upon your families, who have an interest in the covenant. For,

First, If you are God's covenant people, though he may afflict, yet he will never forget you; he is ever mindful of his covenant (*Psa.* 111:5). You are as much upon his heart in your deepest afflictions as in the greatest flourish of your prosperity.

You find it hard to forget your child, though it be now turned to a heap of corruption, and loathsome rottenness; Oh, how does your mind run upon it night and day! your thoughts tire not upon that object: why, surely it is much more easy for you to forget your dear child, whilst living and most endearing (much more when dead and undesirable), than it is for your God to forget you. 'Can a woman forget her sucking child, that she should not have compassion on the son of her womb? yea, they may forget, yet will not I forget you' (*Isa.* 49:15).

Can a woman, the more affectionate sex, *forget her sucking child,* her own child, and not a nursing child? Her own child, whilst it hangs on the breast, and, together with the milk from the breast, draws love from its mother's heart; can such a thing as this be in nature? Possibly it may; for creature-love is fickle, and variable; but, *I will not forget you;* it is an everlasting covenant.

Secondly, As he will never forget you in your troubles, so he will order all your troubles for your good: it is *a well-ordered covenant,* or a covenant orderly disposed; so that every thing shall work together for your good.

The covenant so orders all your trials, so ranks and disposes your various troubles, that they shall, in their orders and places, sweetly co-operate, and join their united influences to make you happy.

Possibly you cannot see how your present affliction should be for your good; you are ready to say, with Jacob, 'Joseph is not, and Simeon is not; and you will take Benjamin away; all these things are against me' (*Gen.* 42:36). But could you once see how sweetly, and orderly all these afflictions work under the blessing and influence of the covenant, to your eternal good, you would not only be quiet but thankful for that which now so much afflicts and troubles you.

Thirdly, This covenant is not only well-ordered in all things, but *sure:* the mercies contained in it are called, 'the sure mercies of David' (*Isa.* 55:3). Now how sweet, how seasonable a support does this consideration give to God's afflicted people under the rod! You lately made yourselves *sure* of that creature-comfort which has forsaken you. It may be you said of your child, which is now gone, as Lamech said of his son Noah, 'This same shall comfort us concerning our work and toil of our hands' (*Gen.* 5:29), meaning that his son should not only comfort them by assisting them in the work of their hands, but also in enjoying the fruit of their toil and pains for him.

Probably such thoughts you have had, and raised up to yourselves great expectations of comfort in your old age from it; but now you see you built upon the sand; and where were you now if you had not a firmer bottom to build upon? But, blessed be God, the covenant-mercies are more sure, and solid! God, Christ, and heaven, never start nor fade, as these things do.

The sweetest creature-enjoyments you ever had or have in this world, cannot say to you, as your God does, 'I will never leave you, nor forsake you.' You must part with your dear husbands, however well you love them; you must bid adieu to the wife of your bosom, however nearly your affections be linked and your heart delight in her. Your children and you must be separated, though they are to you as your own soul.

But though these vanish away, blessed be God, there is something that abides. Though all flesh be as grass, and the beauty of it as the flower of the grass, though the grass withers, and its flower fades, because the Spirit of the Lord blows upon it, yet the word of our God shall stand for ever (*Isa.* 40:6–8). There is so much of support contained in this one consideration that, could but your faith fix here, to realize and apply it, I might lay down my pen at this period, and say, the work is done; there needs no more.

Consideration 9. The hope of the resurrection should powerfully restrain all excesses of sorrow in those that do profess it.

Let them only mourn without measure who mourn without hope. The husbandman does not mourn when he casts his seed-corn into the earth, because he sows in hope. He commits it to the ground with an expectation to receive it again with improvement. Why, thus stands the case here, and just so the apostle states it: 'But I would not have you to be ignorant, brethren, concerning them which are asleep, that you sorrow not, even as others which have no hope. For if we believe that Jesus died and rose again, even so them also which sleep in Jesus will God bring with him' (*1 Thess.* 4:13–14).

That is, look not upon the dead as a lost generation; think not that death has annihilated and utterly destroyed them. Oh no, they are not dead, but only sleep; and if they sleep, they shall awake again. You do not use to make outcries and lamentations for your children, and friends, when you find them asleep upon their beds. Why, death is but a longer sleep, out of which they shall as surely awake as ever they did in the morning in this world.

I have often wondered at that golden sentence in Seneca:

My thoughts of the dead are not as others are; I have fair and pleasant apprehensions of them; for I enjoyed them as one that reckoned he must part with them; and I part with them as one that makes account to have them.[1]

He speaks, no doubt, of that enjoyment of them which his pleasant contemplations of their virtuous actions could give him; for he was wholly unacquainted with the comfortable and heart-supporting doctrine of the resurrection. Had he known the advantages which result thence, at what a rate may we think he would have spoken of the dead, and of their state; but this you profess to believe, and yet sink at a strange rate. Oh, suffer not Gentilism to

---

[1] *Habui enim illos tanquam amissurus, amisi tanquam habeam.* Seneca, Epistle 63.

outvie Christianity; let not Pagans challenge the greatest believers, to outdo them in a quiet and cheerful behaviour under afflictions.

I beseech you, reader, if your deceased friend have left you any solid ground of hope that he died interested in Christ and the covenant, that you will distinctly ponder these admirable supports which the doctrine of the resurrection affords.

First, That the same body that was so pleasant a spectacle to you shall be restored again; yea, the same *numerically,* as well as the same *specifically;* so that it shall not only be *what* it was, but *who* it was. 'These eyes shall behold him, and not another' (*Job* 19:27). The very same body you laid, or are now about to lay, in the grave, shall be restored again. You shall find your own husband, wife, or child, or friend again: I say, the self-same, and not another.

Secondly, And, farther, this is supporting, that as you shall see the same person that was so dear to you; so you shall know them to be the same that were once endeared to you on earth in so near a tie of relation.

Indeed you shall know them no more in any carnal relation; death has dissolved that bond. But you shall know them to be such as once were your dear relations in this world, and be able to single them out among that great multitude, and say, this was my father, mother, husband, wife, or child; this was the person for whom I wept and made supplication, who was an instrument of good to me, or to whose salvation God made me instrumental.

For we may allow, in that state, all that knowledge which is *cumulative* and *perfective,* whatsoever may enlarge and heighten our felicity and satisfaction, as this must needs be allowed to do. Luther's judgment on this point being sought by his friends at supper the evening before he died, he replies thus,

> What [says he] befell Adam? He never saw Eve, but was in a deep sleep when God formed her; yet when he awaked and saw her, he asked not what she was, nor whence she came, but says she was flesh of his flesh, and bone of his bone. Now, how knew he that? He, being full of the Holy Ghost, and endued with the knowledge of God, spoke thus; after the same manner, we also shall be in the other life renewed by Christ, and shall know our parents, our wives, and children.[1]

And this, among other things, was that with which Augustine comforted the lady Italica, after the death of her dear husband, telling her that she should know him in the world to come among the glorified saints.[2] Yea, and a greater than either of these, I mean Paul, comforted himself that the Thessalonians, whom he had converted to Christ, should be 'his joy and crown of rejoicing in the presence of the Lord Jesus Christ at his coming' (1 *Thess.* 2:19–20), which must needs imply his distinct knowledge of them in that day, which must be many hundred years after death has separated them from each other. Whether this knowledge shall be by the glorified eyes discerning any lineaments or property of individuation remaining

---

[1] Melchior Adam, in his *Life of Luther*.
[2] Augustine: Epistle 6.

upon the glorified bodies of our relations; or whether it shall be by immediate revelation, as Adam knew his wife, or as Peter, James, and John, knew Moses and Elijah in the mount; as it is difficult to determine, so it is needless to puzzle ourselves about it.

It is the concurrent judgment of sound divines, and it wants not countenance from Scripture and reason, that such a knowledge of them shall be in heaven; and then the sadness of this parting will be abundantly recompensed by the joy of that meeting. Especially considering,

Thirdly, That at our next meeting, they shall be unspeakably more desirable, sweet, and excellent, than ever they were in this world. They had a desirableness in them here, but they were not altogether lovely, and in every respect desirable; they had their infirmities, both natural and moral; but all these are removed in heaven, and for ever done away: no natural infirmities hang about glorified bodies, or sinful ones upon perfected spirits of the just. Oh what lovely creatures will they appear to you then, when that which is now sown in dishonour, shall be raised in honour (*1 Cor.* 15:43)! And then, to crown all,

Fourthly, You shall have an everlasting enjoyment of them in heaven, never to part again. The children of the resurrection can die no more (*Luke* 20:36); you shall kiss their pale lips and cold cheeks no more; you shall never fear another parting pull, but be together with the Lord for ever (*1 Thess.* 4:17). And this the apostle thought an effectual cordial in this case when he exhorted the Thessalonians to 'comfort one another with these words'.

Consideration 10. *The present felicity into which all that die in Christ are presently admitted should abundantly comfort Christians over the death of such as either carried a lively hope out of the world with them, or have left good grounds of such a hope behind them.*

Such they are that carried a lively hope to heaven with them, who could evidence to themselves and friends, their interest in Christ and in the covenant. Yea, though they had died in silence, yet their conversations would have spoken for them, and the tenor of their lives leave no ground of doubting touching their death. Others dying in their infancy and youth, though they carried not such an actual hope with them, yet have left good grounds of hope behind them.

Parents, now ponder these grounds; you have prayed for them, you have many times wrestled with the Lord on their behalf; you have taken hold of God's covenant for them, as well as for yourselves, and dedicated them to the Lord; and they have not, by any actions of theirs, destroyed those grounds of your hope, but you may, with much probability, conclude they are with God.

Why, if the case be so, what abundant reason have you to be quiet and well satisfied with what God has done? Can they be better than where they are? Had you better provisions and entertainment for them here than their heavenly Father has above ?

There is no Christian parent in the world, but would rejoice to see his child outstrip and get before him in grace, that he may be more eminent in parts and service than ever he was; and what reason can be given why we should not as much rejoice to see our children get before us in glory as in grace? They have got to heaven a few years before you, and is that matter of mourning? Would not your child (if he were not ignorant of you) say, as Christ did to his friends, a little before his death, when he saw them cast down at the thoughts of parting, 'If you loved me, you would rejoice, because I said I go to the Father' (*John* 14:28). That is, do not value your own sensible comfort, from my bodily presence with you, before my glory and advancement in heaven. Is this love to me? Or is it not rather self-love?

So would your departed friend say to you:

You have professed much love all along to me; my happiness seemed to be very dear to you. How comes it to pass, then, that you mourn so exceedingly now? This is rather the effect of a fond and fleshly than of a rational and spiritual love; if you loved me with a pure spiritual love, you would rejoice that I am gone to my Father. It is infinitely better for me to be here, than with you on earth, under sin and sorrow. Weep not for me, but for yourselves.

Alas! though you want your friend's company, he wants not yours; your care was to provide for this child, but Jesus Christ his provided infinitely better for it than you could; you intended an estate, but he a kingdom for it. You thought on such or such a match, but Christ has forbid all others, and married your child to himself. Would you imagine a higher preferment for the fruit of your bodies?

A king from heaven has sent for your friend, and do you grudge at the journey? O think, and think again, what an honour it is to you that Christ has taken them out of your bosom and laid them in his own; stripped them out of those garments you provided, and clothed them in white robes washed in the blood of the Lamb. Let not your hearts be troubled; rather rejoice exceedingly that God made you instruments to replenish heaven and bring forth an heir for the kingdom of God.

Your child is now glorifying God in a higher way than you can, and what though you have lost its bodily presence for a time? I hope you do not reckon that to be your loss which turns to God's greater glory.

When Jacob heard his Joseph was lord of Egypt, he rather wished himself with Joseph than his Joseph with him in wants and straits. So should it be with you. You are yet rolling and tossing upon a tempestuous sea, but your friend is gone into the quiet harbour; desire rather to be there than that he were at sea with you again.

Consideration 11. *Consider how vain a thing all your trouble and self-vexation is; it no way betters your case, nor eases your burden.*

As a bullock, by wrestling and sweating in the furrow, makes his yoke to be more heavy, galls his neck, spends his strength the sooner, and in no way helps himself by that – why thus stands the case with you, if you be as a bullock unaccustomed to the yoke (*Jer.* 31:18). What Christ says of *caring*, we may say of *grieving*, 'Which of you, by taking thought, can add one cubit to his stature?' (*Matt.* 6:27).

Cares may break our sleep, yea, break our hearts, but they cannot add to our stature, either in a natural or in a civil notion; so our sorrowing may sooner break our hearts than the yoke God has laid on you.

Alas! what is all this but as a fluttering of a bird in the net which, instead of freeing, does but the more entangle itself. It was therefore a wise resolution of David in this very case, when the will of God was signified in the death of his child, 'But now he is dead, wherefore should I fast? can I bring him back again? I shall go to him, but he shall not return to me' (2 *Sam.* 12:23).

Can I bring him back again? No, I can no more alter the purpose and work of God than I can change the seasons of the year, or alter the course of the sun, moon, and stars, or disturb the order of the day and night; which are all unalterably established by a firm constitution and ordinance of heaven.

As these seasons cannot be changed by man, so neither can this course and way of his providence be changed. 'He is of one mind, and who can turn him? and what his soul desires, even that he does' (*Job* 23:13). Indeed, while his pleasure and purpose are unknown to us, there is room for fasting and prayer, to prevent the thing we fear; but when the purpose of God is manifested in the issue and the stroke is given, then it is the vainest thing in the world to fret and vex ourselves, as David's servants thought he would do, as soon as he should hear that the child was dead: but he was wiser than to act so, his tears and cries to God before had the nature and use of means to prevent the affliction; but when it was come, and could not be prevented, then they were of no use, to no purpose in the world. 'Wherefore should I fast?', that is, to what end, use, or purpose will it be now?

Well then, cast not away your strength and spirits to no advantage; reserve them for future exercise and trials. Time may come that you may need all the strength you have, and much more, to support greater burdens than this.

Consideration 12. *The Lord is able to restore all your lost comforts in relations double to you, if you meekly submit to him and patiently wait upon him under the rod.*

When Esau had lost his blessing, he said, 'Have you but one blessing, my father?' (*Gen.* 27:38). But your Father has more blessings for you than one; his name is the Father of mercies (2 *Cor.* 1:3). He can beget and create as many mercies for you as he pleases; relations, and the comforts of them, are at his command.

It is but a few months or years past and these comforts, whose loss you now lament, were not in being; nor did you know whence they should arise to you, yet the Lord gave the word, and commanded them for you; and, if he please, he can make the death of these but like a scythe to the meadow that is mown down, or a razor to the head that is shaved bare; which, though it lay you under the present trouble and reproach of barrenness, yet does but make way for a double increase, a second spring with advantage.

So that as it was with the captive church, in respect of her special children, in the day of her captivity and reproach, the Lord made up all with advantage to her, even to her own astonishment. 'The children which you shall have, after you have lost the other, shall say again in your ears, the place is too strait for me; give place to me that I may dwell' (*Isa.* 49:20).

Thus may he deal with you as to your natural children and relations; so that what the man of God said to Amaziah may be applied to the case in hand. 'Amaziah said to the man of God, But what shall we do for the hundred talents? And the man of God answered. The LORD is able to give you much more than this' (2 *Chron.* 25:9).

Oh say not, What shall I do for friends and relations? Death has robbed me of all comfort in them. Why, the Lord is able to give you much more. But then, as ever you expect to see your future blessings multiplied, look to it and be careful that you neither dishonour God nor grieve him by your unsubmissive and impatient carriage under the present rod.

God took away all Job's children, and that at one stroke, and that stroke immediate and extraordinary, and that when they were grown up and planted (at least some of them) in distinct families; yea, whilst they were endearing each other by mutual expressions of affection. This must be granted to be an extraordinary trial, yet he meekly receives and patiently bears it from the hand of the Lord.

You have heard of the patience of Job, says the apostle (*James* 5:11), 'and have seen the end of the Lord.' Not only the gracious end or intention of the Lord in all his afflictions, but the happy end and issue the Lord gave to all his afflictions, of which you have the account in Job 42:10: 'The LORD gave Job twice as much as he had before.' The number of his children was not double to what he had, as all his other comforts were, but though the Lord only restored the same number to him again that he took away, yet it is likely the comforts he had in these latter children were double what he had in the former. There is nothing lost by waiting patiently and submitting willingly to the Lord's disposal.

It is as easy with the Lord to revive as it is to remove your comforts in relations. There is a sweet expression to this purpose in Psalm 18:28: 'For you will light my candle; the LORD my God will enlighten my darkness.'

Every comfortable enjoyment, whether it be in relations, estate, health, or friends, is a candle lighted by providence for our comfort in this world, and they are but candles, which will not always last; and those that last longest will be consumed and wasted at last; but often it falls out with them as with candles, they are blown out before they are half consumed; yea, almost as soon as lighted up; and then we are in darkness for the present.

It is a dark hour with us, when these comforts are put out; but David's faith did, and ours may, comfort us with this, that he that blew out the candle can light up another. 'You shall light my candle, the LORD my God will enlighten my darkness.' That is, the Lord will renew my comforts, alter the present sad state I am in, and chase away that trouble and darkness which at present lies upon me; only beware of offending him, at whose beck your lights and comforts come and go. Michal displeased the Lord, and therefore had no child unto the day of her death (2 *Sam.* 6:23).

Hannah waited humbly upon the Lord for the blessing of children, and the Lord remembered her; he enlightened her condition with that comfort when she was a lamp despised. There is no comfort you have lost but God can restore, yea, double it in kind, if he sees it convenient for you.

Consideration 13. *Consider, though he should deny you any more comforts of this kind, yet he has far better to bestow upon you, such as these deserve not to be named with.*

You have an excellent scripture to that purpose in Isaiah 54:4–5.

> For thus says the LORD unto the eunuchs that keep my sabbaths, and choose the things that please me, and take hold of my covenant; even unto them will I give in mine house and within my walls a place and a name better than of sons and daughters: I will give them an everlasting name, that shall not be cut of.

Men's names are to be continued in their issue, in their male issue especially, and consequently to fail in such as wanted issue (*Num.* 27:4), and a numerous issue is deemed no small honour (*Psa.* 127:4-5). God therefore promised here to supply and make good the want of issue, and whatsoever, either honour here or memorial hereafter, might from it have accrued to them, by bestowing upon them matter of far greater honour and more durable; a name better than or before the name of sons or daughters.

It is a greater honour to be the child of God than to have the greatest honour or comfort that ever children afforded their parents in this world.

Poor heart, you are now dejected by this affliction that lies upon you, as if all joy and comfort were now cut off from you in this world.

A cloud dwells upon all other comforts; this affliction has so embittered your soul that you taste no more in any other earthly comforts than in the white of an egg. Oh that you did but consider the consolations that are with God for such as answer his ends in affliction, and patiently wait on him for their comfort! He has comforts for you far transcending the joy of children.

This some have found when their children have been cut off from them, and that in so eminent a degree that they have little valued their comfort in children in comparison with this comfort.

I will therefore set down a pregnant instance of the point in hand, as I find it recorded by the grave and worthy author of that excellent book entitled, *The Fulfilling of the Scripture* [Robert Fleming (1630-94)]:

> Another notable instance of grace, with a very remarkable passage in his condition, I shall here mention.

One Patrick Mackewrath, who lived in the west parts
of Scotland, whose heart in a remarkable way the Lord
touched, and after his conversion (as he showed to many
Christian friends) was in such a frame, so affected with
a new world wherein he was entered, the discoveries
of God and of a life to come, that for some months
together he did seldom sleep but was still taken up in
wondering. His life was very remarkable for tenderness
and near converse with God in his walk; and, which was
worthy to be noted, one day, after a sharp trial, having
his only son suddenly taken away by death, he retired
alone for several hours, and when he came forth, did
look so cheerfully that to those who asked him the reason thereof, and wondered at the same in such a time,
he told them, He had got that in his retirement with the
Lord that, to have it afterwards renewed, he would be
content to lose a son every day.

Oh, what a sweet exchange had he made! Surely he had
gold for brass, a pearl for a pebble, a treasure for a trifle;
for so great, yea, and far greater is the disproportion between the sweet light of God's countenance, and the faint
dim light of the best creature-enjoyment.

Would it please the Lord to make this sun arise and
shine upon you, now when the stars that shone with a
dim and borrowed light are gone down, you would see
such gain by the exchange as would quickly make you
cast in your votes with him we now mentioned, and say,
Lord, let every day be such as this funeral day; let all my
hours be as this, so that I may see and taste what I now
do. How gladly would I part with the dearest and nearest
creature-comforts I own in this world. The gracious and

tender Lord has his divine cordials reserved on purpose for such sad hours; these are sometimes given before some sharp trial, to prepare us for it, and sometimes after, to support us under it.

I have often heard it from the mouth, and found it in the diary of a sweet Christian now with God, that a little before the Lord removed her dear husband by death, there was such an abundant outlet of the love of God unto her soul for several days and nights following, that when the Lord took away her husband by death, though he was a gracious and sweet-tempered (and by her most tenderly beloved) husband, she was scarce sensible of the stroke, but carried quite above all earthly things, their comforts, and their troubles, so that she almost lost the thoughts of her dear husband in God. And had not the Lord taken that course with her, she concluded that blow had not been possible to be borne by her, she must have sunk without such a preparative.

A husband, a wife, a child, are great, very great things, as they stand by other creatures; but surely they will seem little things, next to nothing, when the Lord shall set himself by them before the soul. And how know you but God has bidden these earthly comforts stand aside this day, to make way for heavenly ones? It may be God is coming to communicate himself more sweetly, more sensibly than ever to your souls; and these are the providences which must cast up and prepare the way of the Lord. Possibly God's meaning in their death is but this: Child, stand aside; you are in my way, and fill my place in your parent's heart.

Consideration 14. *Be careful you exceed not in your grief for the loss of earthly things, considering that Satan takes the advantage of all extremes.*

You cannot touch any extreme but you will be touched by that enemy whose greatest advantages lie in assaulting you here.

Satan is called, *The ruler of the darkness of this world* (*Eph.* 6:12), that is, his kingdom is supported by darkness. Now, there is a twofold darkness which gives Satan great advantage; the darkness of the *mind,* ignorance; and the darkness of the *condition,* trouble and affliction. Of the former, the apostle speaks chiefly in that text; but the latter also is by him often improved, to carry on his designs upon us. When it is a dark hour of trouble with us, then is his fittest season to tempt.

That cowardly spirit falls upon the people of God, when they are down and low in spirit as well as state. Satan would never have desired that the hand of God should have been stretched out upon Job's person, estate, and children but that he promised himself a notable advantage therein, to poison his spirit with vile thoughts of God. 'Do this [says he] and he will curse you to your face.'

What the Psalmist observes of *natural,* is as true of *metaphorical* darkness, 'You make darkness, and it is night, wherein all the beasts of the forest creep forth; the young lions roar after their prey' (*Psa.* 104:20).

When it is dark night with men, it is noon-day with Satan; that is, our suffering-time is his busiest working-time; many a dismal suggestion he then plants and grafts upon our affliction, which are much more dangerous to us than the affliction itself.

Sometimes he injects *desponding* thoughts into the afflicted soul. 'For I said in my haste, I am cut off from before your eyes' (*Psa.* 31:22); 'My hope is perished from the LORD: remembering my affliction and my misery, the wormwood and the gall' (*Lam.* 3:18–19).

Sometimes he suggests *hard* thoughts of God: 'The Almighty has dealt very bitterly with me' (*Ruth* 1:20). Yea, that he has dealt more severely with us than any other; 'Behold, and see if there be any sorrow like unto my sorrow, which is done unto me, wherewith the LORD has afflicted me in the day of his fierce anger' (*Lam.* 1:12).

And sometimes he suggests *murmuring* and *repining* thoughts against the Lord. The soul is displeased at the hand of God upon it. Jonah was angry at the hand of God, and said, 'I do well to be angry, even unto death' (*Jon.* 4:9). What dismal thoughts are these! And how much more afflictive to a gracious soul than the loss of any outward enjoyment in this world.

And sometimes he suggests very *irreligious* and *atheistical* thoughts, as if there were no privilege to be had by religion, and all our pains, zeal, and care about duty, were little better than lost labour: 'Verily I have cleansed my heart in vain, and washed my hands in innocency; for all the day long have I been plagued, and chastened every morning' (*Psa.* 73:13–14).

By these things Satan gets no small advantage upon the afflicted Christian; for albeit these thoughts are his

burden, and God will not impute them to the condemna-
tion of his people, yet they rob the soul of peace, hinder
it from duty, and make it act uncomely under affliction,
to the stumbling and hardening of others in their sin.
Beware, therefore, lest by your excess of sorrow you give
place to the devil. 'We are not ignorant of his devices.'

Consideration 15. *Give not way to excessive sorrows on
account of affliction, if you have any regard to the honour of God and religion, which will hereby be exposed to
reproach.*

If you slight your own honour, do not slight the honour of God and religion too; take heed how you carry it
in a day of trouble; many eyes are upon you. It is a true
observation that a late worthy author has made upon this
case:

> What will the Atheist, and what will the profane scoffer
> say, when they shall see this? So sottish and malicious
> they are, that if they do but see you in affliction, they are
> straightway scornfully demanding, Where is your God?
> But what would they say, if they should hear you your-
> selves unbelievingly cry out, Where is our God? Will
> they not be ready to cry, this is the religion they make
> such boast of, which you see how little it does for them
> in a day of extremity: they talk of promises, rich and
> precious promises; but where are they now? Or to what
> purpose do they serve? They said they had a treasure in
> heaven; what ails them to mourn so then, if their riches
> are there?[1]

[1] Matthew Mead in his *Appendix to Solomon's Prescription*, p. 1, 2.

[82]

Oh, beware what you do before the world. They have eyes to see what you can do, as well as ears to hear what you can say: and as long as your carriage under trouble is so much like their own, they will never think your principles are better than theirs. Carnal worldlings will be drawn to think that whatever fine talk you may have about God and heaven, your hearts were most upon the same things that theirs were, since your grief for their removal is as great as theirs.

They know by experience what a stay it is to the heart to have an able, faithful friend to depend upon, or to have hopes of a great estate shortly to fall to them; and they will never be persuaded you have any such ground of comfort if they see you so much cast down as they who pretend to no such matter. By this means the precepts of Christ to constancy and contentment in all estates will come to be looked upon (like those of the *Stoics*), only as *magnifica verba*, brave words, but such as are impossible to be practised; and the whole of the gospel will be taken for an airy notion, since they that profess greatest regard to it are no more helped thereby.

Oh, what a shame it is that religion should, in this case, make no more difference between man and man! Wherefore show to the world (whatever their common censures are), that it is not so much your care to differ from them in some opinions and a little strictness as in humility, meekness, contempt of the world, and heavenly-mindedness; and now let these graces display themselves by your cheerful, patient deportment under all your grievances.

Wherefore has God planted those excellent graces in your souls but that he might be glorified and you benefited by the exercise of them in tribulation? Should these be suppressed and hid, and nothing but the pride, passion, and unmortified earthliness of your hearts set on work and discovered in the time of trouble, what a slur, what a wound will you give to the glorious name which is called upon by you? And then, if your hearts be truly gracious, that will pierce you deeper than ever your affliction which occasioned it did.

I beseech you, therefore, be tender of the name of God, if you will not be so of your own peace and comfort.

Consideration 16. *Be quiet and hold your peace; you little know how many mercies lie in the womb of this affliction.*

Great are the benefits of a sharp, rousing affliction to the people of God at some times, and all might have them at all times, were they more careful to improve them. Holy David thankfully acknowledges, 'It is good for me that I have been afflicted' (*Psa.* 119:71).

And surely there is as much good in them for you, as for him; if the Lord sanctify them to such ends and uses as his were sanctified unto.

Such a smarting rod as this came not before there was need enough of it, and possibly you saw the need of some awakening providence yourselves; but if not, the Lord did: he took not up the rod to smite you till his faithfulness and tender love to your souls called upon him to correct you.

You now sit pensive under the rod, sadly lamenting and deploring the loss of some earthly comfort; your heart is surcharged with sorrow, your eyes run down upon every mention and remembrance of your dear friend. Why, if there were no more, this alone may discover the need you had of this rod; for does not all this sorrow at parting plainly speak how much your heart was set upon, how fast your heart was glued to this earthly comfort?

Now you see that your affections were sunk many degrees deeper into the creature, than you were aware of, and what should God do in this case by you? Should he suffer you to cleave to the creature more and more? Should he permit it to purloin and exhaust your love and delight, and steal away your heart from himself? This he could not do, and love you. The more impatient you are under this affliction, the more need you had of it.

And what if by this stroke the Lord will awaken your drowsy soul, and recover you out of that pleasant but dangerous spiritual slumber you were fallen into, whilst you had pillowed your head upon this pleasant, sensible creature-enjoyment? Is not this really better for you than if he should say, Sleep on: he is joined to idols, let him alone; he is departing from me, the fountain, to a broken cistern; let him go.

Yea, what if by this stroke upon one of the most pleasant things you had in this world God will discover to you, more sensibly and effectually than ever, the vanity both of that and all earthly comforts, so as that you shall from henceforth never let forth your heart, your hope, your love and delight to any of them as you did before? You could talk before of the creature's vanity; but I question whether ever you had so clear and convincing a sight of its vanity as you have this day; and is not this a considerable mercy in your eyes? Now, if ever, God is weaning you from all fond opinions and vain expectations from this world; by this your *judgment* of the creature is *rectified*, and your *affections* to all other enjoyments on earth *moderated*; and is this nothing? Oh, doubtless it is a greater mercy to you than to have your friend alive again.

And what if by this rod your wandering, gadding heart shall be whipped home to God, your neglected duties revived, your decayed communion with God restored, a spiritual, heavenly frame of heart recovered? What will you say then? Surely you will bless that merciful hand which removed the obstructions and adore the divine wisdom and goodness that, by such a device as this, recovered you to himself. Now you can pray more constantly, more spiritually, more affectionately than before. O blessed rod, which buds and blossoms with such fruits as these! Let this be written among your best mercies, for you will have cause to adore and bless God eternally for this beneficial affliction.

Consideration 17. Suffer not yourselves to be transported by impatience and swallowed up of grief because God has exercised you under a smart rod; for, as smarting as it is, it is comparatively a gentle stroke to what others, as good as yourselves, have felt.

Your dear relation is dead. Be it so. Here is but a single death before you; but others have seen many deaths contrived into one upon their relations, to which yours is nothing.

Zedekiah saw his children murdered before his eyes, and then had those eyes (alas, too late) put out. The worthy author of the excellent book before mentioned[1] tells us of a choice and godly gentlewoman in the north of Ireland who, when the rebellion broke out there, fled with three children, one of them upon the breast. They had not gone far before they were stripped naked by the Irish who, to their admiration, spared their lives (it is like, concluding that cold and hunger would kill them). Afterwards, going on at the foot of a river which runs to Lough Neagh, others met them, and would have cast them into the river; but this godly woman, not dismayed, asked a little liberty to pray, and as she lay naked on the frozen ground, got resolution not to go on her own feet to so unjust a death; upon which, having been called, and she refusing, she was dragged by the heels along that rugged way to be cast in with her little ones and company.

But she then turned, and on her knees says, You should, I am sure, be Christians, and men I see you are; in taking away our miserable lives, you do us a pleasure; but know that, as we never wronged you nor yours, you must remember to die also yourselves, and one day give an account of this cruelty to the Judge of heaven and earth. Hereupon they resolved not to murder them with their

[1] *The Fulfilling of the Scripture.*

own hands, but turned them all naked upon a small island in the river, without any provisions, there to perish.

The next day, the two boys having crept aside, found the hide of a beast which had been killed at the root of a tree, which the mother cast over them, lying upon the snow. The next day a little boat goes by, unto whom she calls for God's sake to take them in, but they, being Irish, refused. She desired a little bread, but they said they had none. Then she begs a coal of fire, which she obtained; and thus, with some fallen chips, made a little fire, and the children, taking a piece of the hide, laid it on the coals, and began to gnaw the leather; but without an extraordinary divine support, what could this do?

Thus they lived ten days without any visible means of help, having no bread but ice and snow, nor drink except water. The two boys being nearly starved, she pressed them to go out of her sight, not being able to see their death; yet God delivered them as miraculously at last as he had supported them all that while.

But judge whether a natural death, in an ordinary way, be comparable to such a trial as this; and yet thus the Lord did by this choice and eminently gracious woman.

And Mr [John] Wall, in his *None but Christ*, relates as sad a passage of a poor family in Germany who were driven unto that extremity in the famine that at last the parents made a motion one to the other to sell one of the children for bread to sustain themselves and the rest; but when they came to consider which child it should be, their hearts so relented, and yearned upon every one, that they resolved rather all to die together. Yea, we read in Lamentations 4:10, 'The hands of the pitiful women have sodden their own children.'

But why speak I of these extremities? How many parents, yea, some godly ones too, have lived to see their children dying in profaneness, and some by the hand of justice, lamenting their rebellion with a rope about their necks?

Ah, reader, little do you know what stings there are in the afflictions of others! Surely you have no reason to think the Lord has dealt more bitterly with you than any. It is a gentle stroke, a merciful dispensation, if you compare it with what others have felt.

Consideration 18. *If God be your God, you have really lost nothing by the removal of any creature-comfort.*

God is the fountain of all true comfort; creatures, the very best and sweetest, are but cisterns to receive and convey to us what comfort God is pleased to communicate to them; and if the cistern be broken, or the pipe cut off, so that no more comfort can be conveyed to us that way, he has other ways and means to do it by, which we think not of; and if he please, he can convey his comforts to his people without any of them. And if he do it more immediately, we shall be no losers by that; for no comforts in the world are so delectable and ravishingly sweet as those that flow immediately from the fountain.

It is the sensuality of our hearts that causes us to affect them so inordinately and grieve for the loss of them so immoderately as if we had not enough in God without these creature supplements.

Is the fullness of the fountain yours? And yet do you cast yourselves down because the broken cistern is removed? The best creatures are no better than cisterns (*Jer.* 2:13). Cisterns have nothing but what they receive, and broken ones cannot hold what is put into them. Why, then, do you mourn as if your life were bound up in the creature? You have as free an access to the fountain as you had before. It is the advice of a heathen (and let them take comfort of it), to repair, by a new earthly comfort, what we have lost in a former.

'You have carried forth him whom you loved,' says Seneca, 'seek one whom you may love in his stead. It is better to repair than to bemoan your loss.'[1]

But if God never repair your loss in things of the same kind, you know he can abundantly repair it himself.

Ah! Christian, is not one kiss of his mouth, one glimpse of his countenance, one seal of his Spirit, a more sweet and substantial comfort than the sweetest relation in this world can afford you? If the stream fail, repair to the fountain; there is enough still; God is where he was, and what he was, though the creature be not.

Consideration 19. *Though you may want a little comfort in your life, yet surely it may be recompensed to you by a more easy death.*

---

[1] *Quem amabas extulisti: quære quem ames. Satius est amicum reparare quam flere*. Seneca: *Epistle* 63.

The removal of your friends before you may turn to your great advantage when your hour is come that you must follow them. Oh, how have many good souls been clogged and ensnared in their dying hour by the loves, cares, and fears they have had about those they must leave behind them in a sinful, evil world!

Your love to them might have proved a snare to you and caused you to hang back, as loath to go hence; for these are the things that make men loath to die. And thus it might have been with you, except God had removed them beforehand, or should give you such sights of heaven, and tastes of divine love as should master and mortify all your earthly affections to these things.

I knew a gracious person (now in heaven) who, for many weeks in her last sickness, complained that she found it hard to part with a dear relation, and that there was nothing proved a greater clog to her soul than this. It is much more easy to think of going to our friends who are in heaven before us than of parting with them and leaving our desirable and dear ones behind us.

And who knows what cares and distracting thoughts you may then be pestered and distracted with upon their account? What shall become of these when I am gone? I am now to leave them, God knows to what wants, miseries, temptations, and afflictions, in the midst of a deceitful, defiling, dangerous world. I know it is our duty to leave our fatherless children and friendless relations with God, to trust them with him that gave them to us; and some have been enabled cheerfully to do so when they were parting from them. Luther could say, 'Lord, you have given me a wife and children, I have little to leave them; nourish, teach, and keep them, O Father of the fatherless, and Judge of the widow.'[1] But every Christian has not a Luther's faith; some find it a hard thing to disentangle their affections at such a time. But now, if God has sent all yours before you, you have so much the less to do; death may be easier to you than to others.

Consideration 20. But if nothing that has been yet said will prevail with you, then, lastly, remember that you are near that state and place which admits no sorrows nor sad reflections upon any such accounts as these.

Yet a little while and you shall not miss them, you shall not need them, but you shall live as the angels of God. We now live partly by faith, partly by sense; partly upon God, and partly upon the creature. Our state is mixed, therefore our comforts are so too. But when God shall be all in all, and we shall be as the angels of God in the way and manner of our living, how much will the case be altered with us then from what it is now!

Angels neither marry nor are given in marriage; neither shall the children of the resurrection; when the days of our sinning are ended, the days of our mourning shall be so too. No graves were opened till sin entered, and no more shall be opened when sin is excluded.

Our glorified relations shall live with us for ever; they shall complain no more, die no more; yea, this is the happiness of

[1] Melchior Adam, in his *Life of Luther*.

that state to which you are passing on that your souls being in the nearest conjunction with God, the fountain of joy, you shall have no concern out of him. You shall not be put upon these exercises of patience nor be subjected to such sorrows as you now feel any more. It is but a little while and the end of all these things will come. Oh, therefore, bear up, as persons who expect such a day of jubilee at hand.

And thus I have finished the second general head of this discourse, which is a dissuasive from the sin of immoderate sorrow.

I now proceed to the third thing proposed — to remove the pleas and excuses for this immoderate grief.

7

Pleas for Immoderate
Grief Answered

*I*t is natural to men, yea, to good men, to justify their
their excesses, or at least to extenuate them, by
pleading for their passions, as if they wanted not
cause and reason enough to excuse them. If these be
fully answered and the soul once convinced and left
without apology for its sin, it is then in a fair way for its
cure, which is the last thing designed in this treatise.

My present business, therefore is, to satisfy those
objections, and answer those reasons which are commonly
pleaded in this case to justify our excessive grief for lost
relations. And though I shall carry it in that line of relation to which the text directs, yet it is equally applicable
to all others.

Plea 1. 'You press me by many great considerations to
meekness and quiet submission under this heavy stroke
of God; but you little know what stings my soul feels
now in it. The child was a child of many prayers; it was a
Samuel begged of the Lord; and I concluded when I had

it that it brought with it the returns and answers of many prayers. But now I see it was nothing less; God had no regard to my prayer about it, nor was it given me in that special way of mercy as I imagined it to be. My child is not only dead, but my prayers in the same day shut out and denied.'

Answer 1. That you prayed for your children before you had them was your duty; and if you prayed not for them submissively, referring it to the pleasure of God to give or deny them, to continue or remove them, as should seem good to him, that was your sin. You ought not to limit the Holy One of Israel, nor prescribe to him, nor negotiate with him for what term you shall enjoy your outward comforts. If you did so, it was your evil, and God has justly rebuked it by this stroke.

If you did pray conditionally, and submissively, referring both the mercy asked and continuance of it to the will of God, as you ought to do, then there is nothing in the death of your child that crosses the true scope and intent of your prayer.

Answer 2. Your prayers may be answered though the thing prayed for be withheld, yea, or though it should be given for a little while, and snatched away from you again. There are four ways of God's answering prayers: by giving the thing prayed for presently (*Dan.* 9:23); or by suspending the answer for a time, and giving it afterwards (*Luke* 18:7); or by withholding from you that mercy which you ask and giving you a much better mercy in the room of it (*Deut.* 3:25, compared with *Deut.* 34:4–5); or, lastly, by giving you patience to bear the loss or want of it (2 *Cor.* 12:9). Now if the Lord has taken away your child, or friend, and in lieu thereof given you a meek, quiet, submissive heart to his will, you need not say he has shut out your cry.

Plea 2. 'But I have lost a lovely, obliging, and most endearing child, one that was beautiful and sweet; it is a stony heart that would not dissolve into tears for the loss of one so desirable, so engaging as this was. Ah! it is no common loss.'

Answer 1. The more lovely and engaging your relation was, the more excellent will your patience and contentment with the will of God in its death be; the more loveliness, the more self-denial, the more grace. Had it been a thousand times more endearingly sweet than it was, it was not too good to deny for God. If therefore obedience to the will of God does indeed master natural affections, so that you look upon patience and contentment as much more beautiful than the sweetest and most desirable enjoyment on earth, it may turn to you for a testimony of the truth and strength of grace: that you can, like Abraham, part with a child whom you so dearly love in obedience to the will of your God, whom you love infinitely more.

Answer 2. The loveliness and beauty of our children and relations, though it must be acknowledged a good gift from the hand of God, yet it is but a common gift, and oftentimes becomes a snare. It is, in its own nature,

[97]

but a transitory, vanishing thing, and therefore no such great aggravation of the loss as is pretended.

I say, it is but a common gift. Eliab, Adonijah, and Absalom had as lovely presences as any in their generation. Yea, it is not only common to the wicked, with the godly, but to the brute animals as well as men, and to most that excel in it, it becomes a temptation; the souls of some had been more beautiful and lovely if their bodies had been less so. Besides, it is but a flower which flourishes in its month and then fades. This, therefore, should not be reflected on as so great a circumstance to aggravate your trouble.

Answer 3. But if your relation sleeps in Jesus, he will appear ten thousand times more lovely in the morning of the resurrection than ever he was in the world. What is the exactest, purest beauty of mortals to the incomparable beauty of the saints in the resurrection? 'Then shall the righteous shine forth as the sun in the kingdom of their Father' (*Matt.* 13:43).

In this hope you part with them; therefore act suitably to your hopes.

Plea 3. 'Oh! but my child was nipped off by death in the very bud; I did but see, and love, and part; had I enjoyed it longer, and had time to suck out of the sweetness of such an enjoyment, I could have borne it more easily; but its months or years with me were so few, that they only served to raise an expectation which was quickly and therefore the more sadly disappointed.'

Answer 1. Did your friend die young, or was the bond of any other relation almost dissolved as soon as made? Let not this seem so intolerable a load to you; for if you have ground to hope they died in Christ, then they lived long enough in this world.[1] It is truly said, that he has sailed long enough who has won the harbour; he has fought long enough who has obtained the victory; he has run long enough who has touched the goal; and he has lived long enough upon earth who has won heaven, be his days here never so few.

Answer 2. The sooner your relation died, the less sin has been committed, and the less sorrow felt: what can you see in this world but sin or sorrow? A quick passage through it to glory is a special privilege. Surely the world is not so desirable a place that Christians should desire an hour's time longer in it for themselves, or theirs, than serves to fit them for a better.

Answer 3. And whereas, you imagine the parting would have been easier if the enjoyment had been longer, it is a fond and groundless suspicion. The longer you had enjoyed them, the stronger would the endearments have been. A young and tender plant may be easily drawn up by a single hand, but when it has spread and fixed its root many years in the earth, it will require many a strong blow and hard tug to root it up. Affections, like those underground roots, are fixed and strengthened by nothing more than by familiarity and long possession; it is much easier parting now than it would be hereafter, whatever

[1] See Richard Baxter's Preface to the *Life of Mr John Janeway*.

you think. However, this should satisfy you, that God's time is the best time.

Plea 4. 'Oh, but I have lost all in one; it is my only one, I have none left in its room to repair the breach and make up the loss. If God had given me other children to take comfort in, the loss had not been so great; but to lose all at one stroke is insupportable.'

Answer 1. Religion allows not unto Christians a liberty of expressing the death of their dear relations by so hard a word as the *loss* of them is; they are not lost, but sent before you.[1] And it is a shameful thing for a Christian to be reproved for such an uncomely expression by a heathen; it is enough to make us blush to read what a heathen said in this case: 'Never say you have lost any thing' (says Epictetus), 'but that it is returned. Is your son dead? He is only restored. Is your inheritance taken from you? It is also returned.' And a while after he adds, εἰ τουτο θεοις φιλον τουτο γινεσθω, that is, 'Let every thing be as the gods would have it.'

Answer 2. It is no fit expression to say you have lost all in one, except that one be Christ; and he, being once yours, can never be lost. Doubtless, your meaning is, you have lost all your comfort of that kind; and what though you have? Are there not multitudes of comforts yet remaining, of a higher kind, and of a more precious and durable nature? If you have no more of that sort, yet, so long as you have better, what cause you have to rejoice!

---

[1] *Non amittuntur sed præmittuntur* (Seneca: *Epistle 63*).

Answer 3. You too much imitate the way of the world in this complaint; they know not how to repair the loss of one comfort but by another of the same nature which must be put up in its room to fill up the vacancy. But have you no other way to supply your loss? Have you not a God to fill the place of any creature that leaves you? Surely, this would better become a man whose portion is in this life than one who professes that God is his all in all.

Plea 5. 'Oh, but my only one is not only taken away, but there remains no expectation or probability of any more. I must now look upon myself as a dry tree, never to take comfort in children any more, which is a cutting thought.'

Answer 1. Suppose what you say is true, that you have no hope nor expectation of another child remaining to you, yet if you have a hope of better things than children, you have no reason to be cast down. Bless God for higher and better hopes than these. In Isaiah 56:5 the Lord comforts them who have no expectations of sons or daughters with this, that he will give unto them in his house and within his walls 'a place and a name better than of sons and daughters'; even 'an everlasting name that shall not be cut off'. There are better mercies and higher hopes than these. Though your hopes of children, or from children, should be cut off, yet if your eternal hopes are secure, and such as shall not make you ashamed, you should not be cast down.

Answer 2. If God will not have your comforts to lie any more in children, then resolve to place them in himself, and you shall never find cause to complain of loss by such an exchange. You will find that in God which is not to be had in the creature; one hour's communion with him, shall give you that which the happiest parent never yet had from his children; you will exchange brass for gold, perishing vanity for solid and abiding excellency.

Plea 6. 'But the suddenness of the stroke is amazing. God gave little or no warning to prepare for this trial. Death executed its commission as soon as it opened it. My dear husband, wife, or child, was snatched unexpectedly out of my arms by a surprising stroke; and this makes my stroke heavier than my complaint.'

Answer 1. That the death of your relation was so sudden and surprising was much your own fault. You ought to have lived in the daily sense of its vanity and expectation of your separation from it; you knew it to be a dying comfort in its best estate, and it is no such wonderful thing to see that dead which you knew before to be dying. Besides, you heard the changes ringing about you in other families; you frequently saw other parents, husbands, and wives, carrying forth their dead. And what were all these, but warnings given to you to prepare for the like trials?

Surely, then, it was your own security and regardlessness that made this affliction so surprising to you; and who is to be blamed for that, you know.

Answer 2. There is much difference between the sudden death of infants and that of grown persons; the latter may have much work to do; many sins actually to repent of, and many evidences of their interest in Christ to examine and clear, in order to their more comfortable death; and so sudden death may be deprecated by them.

But the case of infants who exercise not their reason is far different; they have no such work to do, but are purely passive. All that is done in order to their salvation is done by God immediately upon them; so it comes all to one whether their death be more quick or more slow.

Answer 3. You complain of the suddenness of the stroke, but another will be ready to say, Had my friend died in that manner, my affliction had been nothing to what now it is; I have seen many deaths contrived into one; I saw the gradual approaches of it upon my dear relation, who felt every thread of death as it came on toward him, who often cried with Job, 'Wherefore is light given to him that is in misery, and life unto the bitter in soul; which long for death, but it comes not, and dig for it more than for hid treasures; which rejoice exceedingly, and are glad, when they can find the grave' (*Job* 3:21–22).

That which you reckon the sting of your affliction others would have reckoned a favour and privilege. How many tender parents and other relations who loved their friends as dearly as yourselves have been forced to their knees upon no other errand but this, to beg the Lord to hasten the separation and to put an end to that sorrow which to them was much greater than the sorrow for the dead.

Plea 7. 'You press me to moderation of sorrows, and I know I ought to show it; but you do not know how the case stands with me. There is a sting in this affliction that none feels but myself; and, oh, how intolerable it is now! I neglected proper means in season to preserve life, or miscarried in the use of means. I now see such a neglect, or such a mistake about the means, as I cannot but judge greatly to contribute to that sad loss which I now, too late, lament.

'Oh, my negligence, my rashness, my inconsiderateness! How does my conscience now smite me for my folly, and by this aggravate my burden beyond what is usually felt by others! Had I seasonably applied myself to the use of proper means and kept strictly to such courses and counsels as those that are able and skilful might have pre-scribed, I might now have had a living husband, wife, or child; whereas I am now not only bereaved, but am apt to think I have bereaved myself of them. Surely there is no sorrow like unto my sorrow.'

Answer 1. Though it be an evil to neglect and slight the means ordained by God for recovery of health, yet it is no less evil to ascribe too much to them, or rely too much on them. The best means in the world are weak and ineffec-tual without God's assistance and concurrence; and they never have his assistance or concurrence when his time is come. And that it was fully come in your friend's case is manifest now by the event. So that if your friend had had the most excellent helps the world affords, they would have availed nothing. This consideration takes place only in your case, who see what the will of God is by the issue, and may not be pleaded by any whilst it remains dubious and uncertain, as it generally does in time of sickness.

Answer 2. Do you not unjustly charge and blame yourself for that which is not really your fault or neglect? How far you are chargeable in this case will best appear by comparing the circumstances you are now in with those you were in when your relation was only arrested by sickness, and it was dubious to you what was your duty and best course to take.

Possibly you had observed so many to perish in physicians' hands, and so many to recover without them, that you judged it safer for your friend to be without those means than to be hazarded by them.

Or, if divers methods and courses were prescribed and persuaded to, and you now see your error in preferring that which was most improper and neglecting what was more safe and probable, yet as long as it did not so appear to your understanding at that time, but you followed the best light you had to guide you, it were most unjust to charge the fault upon yourself for choosing that course that then seemed best to you, whether it were so in itself or not.

To be angry with yourself for doing or omitting what was then done or omitted, according to your best discretion and judgment, because you now see it by the light of the event far otherwise than you did before, is to be troubled that you are but a man, or that you are not as God, who only can foresee issues and events; and that you acted as all rational creatures are bound to do, according to the light they have at the time and season of action.

Answer 3. To conclude, times of great affliction are ordinarily times of great temptation, and it is usual with Satan then to charge us with more sins than we are guilty of, and also to make those things to be sins which, upon impartial examination, will not be found to be so.

Indeed, had your neglect or miscarriage been known or voluntary, or had you really preferred a little money (being able to give it) before the life of your relation, and did deliberately choose to hazard this rather than part with that, no doubt, then, but there had been much evil of sin mixed with your affliction; and your conscience may justly smite you for it as your sin; but in the other case, which is more common, and I presume yours, it is a false charge, and you ought not to abet the design of Satan in it.

Judge by the sorrow you now feel by your friend in what degree he was dear to you and what you could now willingly give to ransom his life, if it could be done with money. Judge, I say, by this how groundless the charge is that Satan now draws up against you, and how you are but too ready to yield to the truth of it.

Plea 8. 'But my troubles are upon a higher score and account: my child or friend is passed into eternity, and I know not how it is with his soul; were I sure that my relation were with Christ, I should be quiet; but my fears of the contrary are overwhelming. Oh, it is terrible to think of the damnation of one so dear to me.'

Answer 1. Admit what the objection supposes, that you have real grounds to fear the eternal condition of your dear relation; yet it is utterly unbecoming for you, even in such a case, to dispute with or repine against the Lord.

I do confess it is a sore and heavy trial, and that there is no cause more sad and sinking to the spirit of a gracious person. Their death is but a trifle to this. But yet if you be such as fear the Lord, I think his indisputable sovereignty over them and his distinguishing love and mercy to you should at least silence you in this matter.

First, His indisputable sovereignty over them. 'Who are you, O man, who replies against God?' (*Rom.* 9:20). The apostle speaks in the matters of eternal election and reprobation. What if the Lord will not be gracious to those that are so dear to us? Is there any wrong done to them or us thereby? Aaron's two sons were cut off in the act of sin by the Lord's immediate hand; and yet he held his peace (*Lev.* 10:3). God told Abraham plainly that the covenant should not be established with Ishmael, for whom he so earnestly prayed – *O let Ishmael live before you!* (*Gen.* 17:18) – and he knew that there was no salvation out of the covenant, and yet he sits down silent under the word of the Lord.

Secondly, But if this do not quiet you, yet I think his distinguishing love and mercy to you should do it. Oh, what do you owe to God that root and branch has not been cast together into the fire! That the Lord has given you good hope through grace that it shall be well with you for ever. Let this stop your mouth, and quiet your spirit, though you would have grounds for this fear.

Answer 2. But pray examine the grounds of your fear, whether it may not proceed from the strength of your affections to the eternal welfare of your friend, or from the subtlety of Satan, designing hereby to overwhelm and swallow you up in supposed as well as from just grounds and causes? In two cases it is very probable your fear may proceed only from your own affection, or Satan's temptation.

First, If your relation died young, before he did any thing to destroy your hopes. Or,

Secondly, If grown, and in some good degree hopeful; only he did not in life or at death manifest and give evidence of grace with that clearness you desired.

As for the case of infants in general, it is none of our concern to judge their condition; and as for those who spring from covenanted parents, it becomes us to exercise charity towards them; the Scripture speaks very favourably of them.

And as for the more adult, who have escaped the pollutions of the world, and made conscience of sin and duty, albeit they never manifested what you could desire they had; yet in them, as in young Abijah, may be found 'some good thing toward the Lord' which you never took notice of. Reverence of your authority, bashfulness and shame-facedness, reservedness of disposition, and many other things, may hide those small and weak beginnings of grace that are in children from the observations of their parents. God might see that in them that you never saw; he does not despise the day of small things.

However this be, it is no longer your responsibility; your concern rather is to improve the affliction to your own good than judge and determine their condition, which belongs not to you but to God.

Plea 9. 'Oh, but I have sinned in this relation, and God has punished my sin in dissolving it. Oh,' says one, 'my heart was set too much upon it, I even idolized it, that was my sin'; and says another, 'I wanted due affections, and did not love my relation, at least not so spiritually as I ought; that was my sin. Now God is visiting me for all the neglects and defects that have been in me towards my relation.'

Answer 1. There is no man so thoroughly sanctified as not to fail and come short in many things pertaining to his relative duties; and, to speak as the thing is, the corruptions of the holiest persons are as much discovered in this as in any other thing whatsoever; and it is a very common thing for conscience, not only to charge these failures upon us, but to aggravate them to the utmost when God has made the separation. So that this is no more than what is usual and very common with persons in your case.

Answer 2. Admit that which the objection supposes, that God had afflicted you for your sin, and removed that comfort from you which you idolized and too much doted on; yet there is no reason you should be so cast down under your affliction; for all this may be and probably is the fruit of his love to and care of your soul. He tells the afflicted, for their comfort, 'As many as I love, I rebuke and chasten' (*Rev.* 3:19). How much better it is to have an idolized enjoyment taken from you in mercy than if God should say concerning you as he did of Ephraim, 'He is joined to idols, let him alone.'

Oh, it is better for you that your Father now reckons with you for your follies with the rod in his hand than to say as he does to some, 'Let them go on, I will not hinder them in or rebuke them for their sinful courses, but will reckon with them for all together in hell at last.'

Answer 3. And as to what you now charge upon yourself, that the spring of your neglect of duty was a want of love to your relation, your sorrow at parting may evidence that your relation was rooted deeply in your affection. But if your love was not so spiritual and pure as to love and enjoy them in God: that was undoubtedly your sin, and is the sin of most Christians, for which both you and all others ought to be humbled.

Plea 10. 'God has blessed me with an estate and outward comforts in the world which I reckoned to have left to my posterity; and now I have none to leave it with, nor have I any comfort to think of it; the purposes of my heart are broken off and the comfort of all my other enjoyments blasted by this stroke in an hour. How are the pains and cares of many years perished.'

Answer 1. How many are there in the world, yea, of our own acquaintance, whom God has either denied or deprived of the comforts both of children and of estates too? If he has left you those outward comforts, you ought to acknowledge his goodness therein, and not to slight these because he has deprived you of the other.

Answer 2. Though your children are gone, yet God has many children left in the world, whose bowels you may refresh with what he has bestowed upon you; and your charity to them will doubtless turn to a more considerable account than if you had left a large estate to your own posterity.

Surely we are not sent into this world to heap up great estates for our children; and if you have been too eager in this design, you may now read God's just rebuke of your folly. Bless God you have yet an opportunity to serve him eminently by your charity, and if God deny you other executors, let your hands be your executors, to distribute to the necessity of the saints, that the blessings of them that are ready to perish may come upon you.

Plea 11. 'Oh, but the remembrance of my child's witty words and pretty actions, is wounding.'

Answer 1. Let it rather lift up your hearts to God in praise that he gave you so desirable a child than fill your heart with discontent at his hand in removing it. How many parents are there in the world whose children God has deprived of reason and understanding, so that they only differ from the beasts in external shape and figure? And how many often show so perverse a temper that little comfort can be expected from them?

Answer 2. These are but small circumstances, and trivial things in themselves; but by these little things Satan manages a great design against your soul, to deject or exasperate it; and surely this is not your business at this time; you have greater things than the words and actions of children to mind. To search out God's ends in the affliction, to mortify the corruption it is sent to rebuke, to quiet your hearts in the will of God; this is your work.

Plea 12. *Lastly,* It is objected, 'Oh, but God hides his face from me in my affliction; it is dark within as well as without; and this makes my case most deplorable, greatly afflicted and sadly deserted.'

Answer 1. Though you want at present sensible comfort, yet you have reason to be thankful for gracious supports. Though the light of God's countenance shine not upon you, yet you find the everlasting arms are underneath you; the care of God works for you when the consolations of God are withdrawn from you.

Answer 2. To have God hide his face in the time of trouble is no new or unusual thing. God's dearest saints, yea, his own Son, have experienced it.

The Son of God, in the deeps of inward and outward trouble, when wave called unto wave, felt not those sweet, sensible influences of comfort from God which had always filled his soul formerly. If Christ cry in extremity, 'My God, my God, why have you forsaken me?', then surely we need not wonder, as if some strange thing had happened to us.

Answer 3. May not your unsubmissive carriage under the rod provoke God to hide his face from you? Pray consider it well: nothing is more probable than for this to be the cause of God's withdrawal from you. Could you, in meekness and quietness, receive that cup your Father has given you to drink; accept the punishment of your iniquities; say, Good is the word of the Lord; It is the Lord, let him do what he will; you would soon find the case altered with you; but the comforting Spirit finds no delight or rest in a turbulent and tumultuous breast.

And thus I have satisfied the most considerable pleas urged in justification of our excesses.

8

Rules to Restrain
Excessive Sorrow

I come to the last thing proposed, namely, the means of curing and preventing these sinful excesses of sorrow for the death of our dear relations.

And although much has been said already to dissuade from this evil, and I have enlarged already much beyond my first intention, yet I shall cast in some further help and assistance towards the healing of this distemper by prescribing the following rules:

Rule 1. If you would not mourn excessively for the loss of creature-comforts, then beware that you set not your delight and love excessively or inordinately upon them whilst you do enjoy them.

Strong affections make strong afflictions; the higher the tide the lower the ebb. According to the measure of our delight in the enjoyment, so is our grief in the loss of these things. The apostle knits these two graces, *temperance* and *patience*, together in the precept in 2 Peter 1:6, and it is very observable how intemperance and impatience are inseparably linked in experience, yea, the experience of the best men. You read, Genesis 37:3, 'Now Israel loved Joseph more than all his children, because he was the son of his old age: and he made him a coat of many colours.'

This was the darling. Jacob's heart was exceedingly set upon him, his very life was bound up in the life of the lad. Now, when the supposed death of the child was brought to him, how did he carry it? See in verses 34–35,

> And Jacob rent his clothes, and put sackcloth upon his loins, and mourned for his son many days: And all his sons and all his daughters rose up to comfort him; but he refused to be comforted; and he said, For I will go down into the grave to my son mourning. Thus his father wept for him.

Here, as in a glass, are the effects of excessive love to a child represented. Here you may see what work immoderate love will make, even in a sanctified heart.

Oh, therefore, let your moderation be known to all men in your delight and sorrows about earthly things; for ordinarily the proportion of the one is answerable to the other.

Rule 2. If you would not be overwhelmed with grief for the loss of your relations, be exact and careful in discharging your duties to them while you have them.

The testimony of your conscience that you laboured in all things to discharge the duties you owed to your relations whilst they were with you will prove an excellent alleviation of your sorrows for them when they are no longer yours. It is not so much the affliction alone as the guilt charged upon us in times of affliction that makes our load so heavy.

Oh, what a terrible thing it is to look upon our dead friends, whilst conscience is accusing and upbraiding us for our duties neglected, and such or such sins committed! Oh, you little think how dreadful a spectacle this will make the dead body of your friend to you!

Conscience, if not quite stupid or dead, will speak at such a time. Oh, therefore, as ever you would provide for a comfortable parting at death, or meeting again at judgment, be exact, punctual, and circumspect in all your relative duties.

Rule 3. If you would not be overwhelmed with trouble for the loss of dear relations, turn to God under your trouble and pour out your sorrows by prayer into his bosom.

This will ease and allay your troubles. Blessed be God for the ordinance of prayer! How much are all the saints beholden to it at all times, but especially in heart-sinking and distressful times! It is some relief when, in distress, we can pour out our trouble into the bosom of a wife, or faithful friend; how much more when we leave our complaint before the gracious, wise, and faithful God! I told you before of that holy man who, having lost his dear and only son, got to his closet, there poured out his soul freely to the Lord, and when he came down to his friends that were waiting below to comfort him and fearing how he would bear that stroke, he came from his duty with a cheerful countenance, telling them he would be content to bury a son, if it were possible, every day, provided he might enjoy such comfort as his soul had found in that private hour.[1]

Go your way, Christian, to your God, get you to your knees in the cloudy and dark day; retire from all creatures, that you may have your full liberty with your God, and there pour out your heart before him, in free, full, and brokenhearted confessions of sin. Judge yourself worthy of hell, as well as of this trouble. Justify God in all his smarting strokes. Beg him, in this distress, to put under you the everlasting arms; entreat one smile, one gracious look, to enlighten your darkness and cheer your drooping spirit.

Say, with the prophet, 'Be not a terror to me: you are my hope in the day of evil' (*Jer.* 17:17). And try what relief such a course will afford you. Surely, if your heart be sincere in this course, you shall be able to say with that holy man, Psalm 94:19, 'In the multitude of my thoughts within me your comforts delight my soul.'

Rule 4. If you would bear the loss of your dear relations with moderation, eye God in the whole process of the affliction more, and secondary causes and circumstances of the matter less.

'I was dumb, I opened not my mouth; because you did it' (*Psa.* 39:9). Consider the hand of the Lord in the whole

[1] See pp. 76–7.

matter, particularly:

First, As a sovereign hand, which has right to dispose of you and all your comforts, without your leave or consent (*Job* 33:13).

Secondly, As a father's hand, correcting you in love and faithfulness. 'Whom the Lord loves he corrects, as a father the son in whom he delights' (*Prov.* 3:12). Oh, if once you could but see affliction as a rod in a father's hand, proceeding from his love, and intended for your eternal good, how quiet you would then be!

And surely if it draws your heart nearer to God, and mortifies it more to this vain world, it is a rod in the hand of special love. If it end in your love to God, doubt not but it comes from God's love to you.

Thirdly, As a just and righteous hand. Have you not procured this to yourself by your own folly? Yea, the Lord is just in all that is come upon you; whatever he has done, he has done you no wrong.

Fourthly, As a moderate and merciful hand that has punished you less than your iniquities deserve. He that has cast you into affliction might justly have cast you into hell. It is of the Lord's mercy that you are not consumed. Why does a living man complain (*Lam.* 3:39)?

Rule 5. If you will bear your affliction with moderation, compare it with the afflictions of other men, and that will greatly quiet your spirits.

You have no cause to say that God has dealt bitterly with you, and that there is no sorrow like your sorrow.

Look round about you, and impartially consider the condition that others are in, and they nothing inferior to you in any respect. You had one dear child; Aaron had two at a stroke, Job all at one stroke; and both of these by an immediate stroke from the hand of God. Some godly parents have lived to see their children die in their sin by the hand of justice, others have seen them live to the dishonour of God, and the breaking of their own spirits, and would have esteemed it a mercy if they had died from the womb and given up the ghost when they came out of the belly, as Job speaks.

In what misery have some parents seen their children lie! God holding them as so many terrible spectacles of misery before their eyes; so that they begged the Lord, with importunity, to let loose his hands, and cut them off; death being, in their esteem, nothing to those continual agonies in which they have seen them lie weltering from day to day. Oh! you little know what a bitter cup others have been given to drink! Surely, if you compare, you must say, 'The Lord has dealt gently and graciously with me.'

Rule 6. Carefully shun and avoid whatsoever may renew your sorrow, or provoke you to impatience.

Increase not your sorrow by the sight of or discourses about sad objects; and labour to avoid them, as occasions presented by the enemy of your souls to draw forth the corruptions of your heart.

I told you before why Jacob would not have the child

of which Rachel died called after the name his wife had given, *Benoni*, the son of my sorrow, lest it should prove a daily occasion of renewing his trouble for the loss of his dear wife; but he called his name *Benjamin*.

Your impatience is like tinder, or gunpowder: so long as you can prevent the sparks from falling on it, there is no great danger; but you that carry such dangerous prepared matter in your own hearts cannot be too careful to prevent them.

Do with murmuring what you do with blasphemous thoughts; think quite another way, and give no occasion.

Rule 7. In the day of your murmuring for the death of your friends, seriously consider your own death as approaching, and that you and your dead friend are distinguished by a small interval and point of time: 'I shall go to him' (2 Sam. 12:23).

Surely the thoughts of your own death as approaching also will greatly allay your sorrows for the dead that are gone before you.

We are apt to fancy a long life in the world, and then the loss of those comforts which we promised ourselves so much of the sweetness and comforts of our lives from is an intolerable thing.

But if you would realize your own death more, you would not be so deeply concerned for their deaths as you are. Could you but look into your own graves more seriously, you would be able to look into your friend's grave more composedly.

And thus I have finished what I designed from this scripture. The Father of mercies and God of all comfort, whose sole prerogative it is to comfort them that are cast down, write all his truths upon your hearts, that they may abide there, and reduce your disordered affections to that frame which best suits the will of God, and the profession you make of subjection and resignation to it.